THE PRENTICE HALL
ESL Workbook

Second Edition

Susan K. Miller
Mesa Community College

with Karen N. Standridge
Pikes Peak Community College

PEARSON

Prentice
Hall

Upper Saddle River, NJ 07458

© 2006 by PEARSON EDUCATION, INC.
Upper Saddle River, New Jersey 07458

10 9 8 7 6 5 4 3

ISBN 0-13-194759-1

Printed in the United States of America

CONTENTS

TO THE STUDENT

Use this workbook along with your English textbook to improve your English grammar skills. You might use this book on your own as a supplement to what you are doing in class, or your teacher might assign specific chapters and exercises for you. in addition, you might work through some of the chapters on your own to improve your understanding and use of English grammatical rules. The more you practice, the more you will remember the grammatical rules.

This book has five major sections:

- **Explanations** of grammatical points
- **Exercises** to practice the grammatical points
- **Appendix A:** Internet Resources
- **Appendix B:** Answer Key
- **Appendix C:** Glossary

You may choose which grammar points to study, or your instructor may recommend some exercises for you to do. For example, you may want to begin with the sentence exercises and then move to the paragraph exercises. You may write directly in this workbook as the directions state, or you may copy the sentences into your own notebook. Copying can help you improve your understanding of English sentences. Working on grammar skills will also help you improve your writing skills, especially if you consistently practice applying your new knowledge with the "Editing in Context" exercises. Remember that it takes time to improve so be patient and persistent.

At the end of each part of the book, you will find an activity called "Editing in Context" that will ask you to apply what you have learned. If you are using this book as a supplement in a writing class, you could practice your new editing skills with assignments from the class. Otherwise, you could practice editing anything you have written. This practice will help you understand and apply grammar rules in your written English. When you are editing your own work, use the following guidelines to help you practice these skills:

1. Use a pen or pencil to point to each word as you read, focusing your attention so that your eyes don't move ahead to the next word or sentence.

2. Try starting at the end of the document, focusing on each sentence in reverse order. This will help you focus on the grammatical points instead of the content of your writing.

3. Try reading the document out loud to get a different perspective on your writing. You might even have someone else read the writing out loud to you.

4. If you are editing something you wrote recently, try to set the writing aside for awhile so that you can edit the piece more objectively.

PART I

N O U N S

■ ■ ■

CHAPTER 1
Singular and Plural

Nouns are words used to name people, places, or things. Nouns are singular if they refer to one person, place, or thing and plural if more than one. It is important to master the ability to use the singular and plural forms of nouns. Some nouns form the plural by adding *-s* or *-es*. Other nouns have irregular plural forms. The explanations and examples below will help you understand the singular and plural forms of nouns.

■ Most *nouns* form the *plural* by adding *-s* or *-es*:

Singular	Plural
table	tables
key	keys
pitch	pitches
kiss	kisses

■ *Nouns* which end in a *consonant + y* form the *plural* by changing *y* to *i* and adding *-es*:

Singular	Plural
lady	ladies
party	parties

- *Irregular nouns* do not follow specific rules. Instead they change their root or their ending. Some common irregular nouns are:

Singular	Plural
child	children
man	men
woman	women
foot	feet
mouse	mice

CHAPTER 2
Count and Noncount

Besides singular and plural nouns, there are *count* and *noncount* nouns. Some nouns are the names of people, places, and things that can be counted. In other words, they can be separated into their parts, granules, pieces, or the like, and those basic elements then can be counted as in one, two, three. These count nouns include words such as pens, rocks, tears, houses, and shoes. Count nouns can be singular or plural. Other nouns are names of things that cannot be counted, that is, separated into their pieces, and these are called *noncount nouns*. Noncount nouns are treated as singular. Some categories of noncount nouns follow:

Category	Examples
Abstract Ideas:	understanding, love, hate, intelligence, advice, knowledge, information, faithfulness, honor, peace, laundry, time (Example: Knowledge opens many doors.)
Activities:	tennis, bowling, homework, writing
Liquids:	oil, blood, milk, water, coffee
Gases:	oxygen, steam
Diseases:	cancer, pneumonia, flu
School subjects:	mathematics, history, English, geometry, social studies
Food:	bread, rice, lettuce, cereal, tea
Natural elements:	rain, snow, wind, weather, thunder

- Some nouns may be *countable* or *noncountable* depending how they are used:

  Time flies so quickly. (noncount)

  In **times** like these, we must demand the truth. (count)

  Many fear **death**. (noncount)

  Over 100 **deaths** occurred during the hurricane. (count)

- Count nouns following the expression "one of" are always in the plural form:

  One of the things I like best about you is your sense of humor.

- When you learn a new noun in English, you should learn whether it is a count or a noncount noun. You can find this information in several different dictionaries, especially those that are written for English language learners.

EXERCISE 1

Underline all of the nouns in the following sentences and then identify if the nouns are count or noncount nouns by placing them in the correct column in the table.

1. One student in my class likes to climb mountains.

2. She claims that mountain climbing helps develop her strength and courage.

3. During her vacation last summer, she climbed a 14,000-ft. peak.

4. After her trip, she wrote about the climb in her journal.

5. Students who read her writing commented on how much her English had improved since last year.

COUNT	NONCOUNT

EXERCISE 2

A. Underline the correct singular or plural noun in sentences 1–15.

B. Go back through sentences 1–15 and use the other word in parenthesis (the word you did not select in Exercise 1.2A). In most cases, you will need to add or delete articles or pronouns to make the sentence correct.

Example: Watching television is a popular (form, forms) of entertainment in America.
Watching television is **one of the** popular **forms** of entertainment in America.

1. Some (program, programs) on television offer viewers opportunities to travel.

2. Viewers can travel around the world without leaving (home, homes).

3. Travel programs are on (television, televisions) every day.

4. (Viewer, Viewers) can learn about foreign places.

5. For example, viewers can learn about the people of other (country, countries) such as Japan, Italy, or Costa Rica.

6. Viewers also can learn some of the traditional (custom, customs) of the people.

7. One travel program explained how the Chinese celebrate (birthday, birthdays).

8. Another program showed German (family, families) preparing several of their favorite meals.

9. Viewers enjoy comparing other (tradition, traditions) with their own traditions.

10. In addition, viewers can see beautiful (thing, things) in nature on travel programs.

11. They may see a (mountain, mountains) in Canada.

12. They may see colorful (bird, birds) in the Philippines.

13. Viewers may even see (lion, lions) in Africa.

14. These sights open their (eye, eyes) to new and wonderful worlds.

15. Watching (television, televisions) helps viewers learn about the world.

Exercise 3

Underline the correct singular or plural noun in the parenthesis.

Example: On the tour, we see **a famous building** like the Empire State Building. (Notice that we have to add the article "a" and delete "the Chrysler Building" because now the sentence is talking about only one place.)

Some TV travel programs take us to [1](place, places) in the United States. For example, one program guides us on a [2](tour, tours) of New York City. On the tour, we see famous [3](building, buildings) like the Empire State Building and the Chrysler Building. Many [4](tourist, tourists) take the elevator to the top of the Empire State Building. How can so many people fit in the [5](elevator, elevators)? The Statue of Liberty stands tall in the harbor welcoming all [6](visitor, visitors) to the United States of America. The statue is located on an [7](island, islands) in the harbor. Many large and small [8](boat, boats) travel around the island. A large passenger boat takes people from the [9](city, cities) to the island. Next, the [10](program, programs) takes us to Times Square. Every New Year's Eve, [11](thousand, thousands) of people gather to celebrate. They watch a lighted ball drop to signify the [12](end, ends) of the year. During the last ten [13](second, seconds), everyone counts together, "Ten, nine, eight, seven, six, five, four, three, two, one! Happy New Year!" Times Square is always a busy [14](place, places).

Another program takes us on a tour of the Nevada [15](desert, deserts). Most of the desert has no [16](plant, plants) and no color. Everything looks like the [17](color, colors) of sand. However, we learn that part of the desert is a bright [18](color, colors). For example, in the Valley of Fire State Park, large red rocks form sculptures that reach toward the [19](sky, skies). Some of the rocks look like giant [20](animal, animals). One is called The Elephant because of its [21](shape, shapes). Three people can sit on top of The Elephant [22](rock, rocks). These are two [23](example, examples) of interesting travel programs about places in the United States.

EXERCISE 4

A. Underline the correct singular or plural noun.

Other travel shows tell about popular tourist [1](attraction, attractions). People of all ages like to watch these [2](show, shows), especially the ones about zoos. Children love to see the variety of [3](animal, animals) at the zoo. In the program about the Washington Zoo, two Panda [4](bear, bears) are eating bamboo. Several [5](lion, lions) are sitting in the sun and eating grass. An [6](owl, owls) blinks his big eyes making the children laugh. All the baby animals at the petting zoo are drinking milk from baby [7](bottle, bottles).

[8](Teenager, Teenagers) also enjoy programs about zoos. Young [9](man, men) and women may want to see more of the snakes and other reptiles at the San Diego Zoo. The narrator carefully explains the difference between a poisonous and nonpoisonous [10](snake, snakes). Young [11](woman, women) and men will also enjoy the segment about birds. The program shows the male peacock dancing in front of a [12](female, females). His [13](feather, feathers) are absolutely beautiful. Also, the segment about the way [14](bat, bats) navigate fascinates all teens.

The long necks and long eyelashes of the giraffes fascinate children, parents, and [15](grandparent, grandparents). The [16](program, programs) about the Milwaukee Zoo makes everyone smile. A monkey swings through his [17](cage, cages). Then he waves at each [18](camera, cameras). This [19](time, times), everyone laughs aloud. All viewers love to see the [20](animal, animals). After watching a travel program about zoos, viewers want to plan a [21](trip, trips) to a zoo soon.

B. For each of the numbered words you selected, explain the reason for your choice.

Example: In (2) the word "these" tells us to use a plural.

(1) _____

(2) _____

(3) _____

(4) _____

(5) _____

(6) _____

(7) _____

(8) _____

(9) _____

(10) _____

(11) _____

(12) _____

(13) _____

(14) _____

(15) _____

(16) _____

(17) _____

(18) _____

(19) _____

(20) _____

(21) _____

EXERCISE 5

A. Write the correct singular or plural form of the noun given in parenthesis, and in the small blanks before the sentences, write *count* or *noncount* to describe the way the noun is being used in the sentence.

B. In some of the sentences, it is possible to change the noun to the other form. Find the sentences whose nouns could be changed and change them, making other changes to the sentence as needed. For example, in sentence 1, you could write "No" for no change or you could change it to ". . . to do their homework assignments." In this case, since homework is a noncount noun, the only way we can change it is to add a limiting word like "assignments" and use the noun as an adjective.

Example: <u>*Noncount*</u> Parents like to give their children lots of (advice) *advice.*

_____ 1. Parents tell young children to do their (homework) _____.

_____ 2. (Mathematics) _____ requires many hours of study.

_____ 3. Some children enjoy doing math (problem) _____.

_____ 4. Other children prefer studying (science) _____.

_____ 5. Some (child) _____ don't want to study at all.

_____ 6. Parents must remind them to study every (day) _____.

_____ 7. Parents also teach their children to do their (laundry) _____.

_____ 8. Kids don't like to pick up their (clothes) _____.

_____ 9. Kids leave their (shoe) _____ and (sock) _____ on the floor.

_____ 10. They also leave their (toy) _____ on the floor.

_____ 11. Parents tell their children, "Pick up your (thing) _____. Your room is a mess."

_____ 12. (Responsibility) _____ is another thing parents teach their children.

_____ 13. Everyone must be responsible for his or her (possession) _____.

_____ 14. Parents want their children to respect people's (property) _____.

_____ 15. Teaching children good (habit) _____ takes time and love.

EXERCISE 6

A. Write the correct singular or plural form of the noun given in parentheses.

B. Explain on a numbered sheet of paper why you have used a singular or plural form.

Examples: 1. More than one individual, so use "*individuals.*"

2. The verb is "*love,*" so it is "*parents love,*" not "*parents loves.*"

C. On a separate sheet of paper, answer the following questions about Exercise 6 after you have done parts A and B.

1. In the first sentence, does the word "other" help you to determine whether the word is singular or plural? Can "other" be used for either singular or plural? Give an example using it with a singular noun.
2. For the noun in blank 8, what other clue is there in the sentence that helps you decide whether the noun is singular or plural?
3. What clue in the sentence tells you that the noun in 4 is singular?
4. What clue in the sentence tells us that the noun in 16 is singular?

D. Go back through the exercise and substitute a synonym for each word given to you in parentheses. For example, in 1, you could use people or persons or human beings.

Caring about other (individual) [1] _____ is an important part of our lives. In the beginning, our (parent) [2] _____ love us unconditionally. They show us (affection) [3] _____ and fulfill all our needs. A mother's understanding (nature) [4] _____ signifies love. A father who teaches his child how to play ball shows (love) [5] _____. We return that love with smiles, hugs, (kiss) [6] _____ and thank yous. Sometimes we do little (thing) [7] _____ for Mom and Dad. Sometimes we give them (card) [8] _____ or presents. Later we learn more about love. We learn to love others who are not members of our (family) [9] _____. As we get older, our (feeling) [10] _____ mature. One (day) [11] _____ we may find a special person to love in a new way. We may even become life (partner) [12] _____. (Trust) [13] _____ and commitment will be

11

important to this relationship. When (child) [14] _____ arrive, the cycle begins again. We open our hearts to the new (generation) [15] _____.

This beautiful (process) [16] _____ will go on until the end of (time) [17] _____.

Editing in Context—Nouns

1. Choose a paragraph that you have written in English recently. It might be something you wrote in a journal, in a letter, for a homework assignment, or for an essay.
2. Underline all nouns in the paragraph, noting whether each is a count or noncount noun. You might even mark each noun with a "C" (count) or an "NC" (noncount).
3. Examine how you have used the noun in the sentence. Should it be singular or plural? Mark any corrections you should make.

PART II

ARTICLES

Articles are often challenging to ESL students because many other languages do not have a part of grammar comparable to them. In other languages that do have articles, the use of articles often differs from the rules of English. The articles **a**, **an**, and **the** are determiners signaling a noun will follow. The noun may have several modifiers and these words may change the article.

Example: I'd like **an** apple. I'd like **a** bright red apple.

The following rules regarding article usage will help you use articles correctly in English:

o   Use **a**, **an**, or **the** with singular count nouns:

- **a** book, **an** orange, **the** chair

o   Usually, place **a** or **an** before nonspecific nouns and **the** before specific nouns:

- We went on **a** vacation to **the** Rocky Mountains.
- On **a** clear day, we could see snow on **the** mountains.
- Henry wants **a** pizza. He likes **the** pizza I make.
- I want **an** egg for breakfast. Please scramble **the** egg for me.

o   Use **a** for first mention of a noun and **the** for second mention of the same noun, once the noun is identified:

- I saw **a** good television show last night. **The** television show was about animal care in zoos.

o   Use **the** before plural count nouns:

- **The** restaurants close early in **the** months of December and January.

o   Adjectives usually *follow* articles:

- **The** beautiful bird sat in **a** tall tree.
- **The** new manager uses **an** old desk.

o   Use **the** with superlative nouns:

- This is **the** best pizza I've ever eaten!

- o Noncount nouns frequently do not require determiners:
    - ◾ I drink coffee for breakfast. My brother drinks juice.
- o Do not use **the** before gerunds. Gerunds are nouns formed by combining a verb with -ing:
    - ◾ Swimming keeps the muscles toned, and eating healthy food keeps the mind focused.
- o Do not use the article **the** before most proper nouns. Proper nouns are nouns that name specific people, places, or things:
    - ◾ Bob is my boyfriend. NOT: The Bob is my boyfriend.
    - ◾ We visited Mexico last summer. NOT: We visited the Mexico last summer.
    - ◾ Our family celebrates Ramadan. NOT: Our family celebrates the Ramadan.
- o Do not use articles before most abstract nouns:
    - ◾ Friendship is very important to me. NOT: The friendship is very important to me.
- o You may use an article before an abstract noun if you are referring to a specific instance or use of the noun, however:
    - ◾ The friendship that I share with Lisa is very important to me.

EXERCISE 7

A. Write the correct article, **a**, **an**, or **the**, in each blank.

B. Look at sentences 1, 2, 8, and 17. Did you use the same article in all the sentences? Should you have? What was the clue? Write a rule to help you remember this use of the article.

C. In sentence number 7, the article is also used in an idiomatic expression. What is the clue? Is this expression almost always used in this way? Write two sentences of your own using this idiomatic expression.

Example: American homes usually have <u>a</u> television in <u>the</u> family room.

1. Many families turn on _____ television when they get out of bed in _____ morning.
2. Stations know that many children watch television in _____ morning.
3. Stations offer _____ series of cartoon programs or family shows.
4. For example, many children enjoy _____ old cartoons featuring Mickey Mouse.
5. Children also like to watch _____ happy world of Mr. Rogers.
6. Mr. Rogers talks to children in _____ gentle way.
7. He teaches them _____ lot about being kind.
8. Adults also enjoy television in _____ morning.
9. _____ adult may watch _____ news and weather.
10. Others enjoy watching _____ cooking show.
11. Some adults love watching _____ interesting talk show.
12. However, not everyone likes all of _____ morning talk shows.
13. Some people do not like _____ problems people discuss.
14. For example, one guest talked about _____ old friend's drug problem.
15. Another guest told her mother's secret to _____ television audience.
16. Some viewers prefer _____ talk show about local events.
17. Television stations show what people want to watch in _____ morning.

15

EXERCISE 8

A. Write **a**, **an**, or **the** in each blank.

B. 1. Explain why the articles for sentences number 1 and 2 are different although the word after the blank in each is the same. What is your clue?

_____

_____

2. In blank 5, what clue tells you which article to use?

_____

3. Explain why you used the articles that you did in sentences number 9, 11, and 13.

_____

_____

Some adults wait until ⁽¹⁾_____ afternoon to watch television. Many people like to watch ⁽²⁾_____ afternoon drama called ⁽³⁾_____ soap opera or "soaps." Soaps are about ⁽⁴⁾_____ lives and affairs of men and women. Each drama usually presents many stories. Some stories focus on ⁽⁵⁾_____ mistakes people make at work or in their personal lives. Other stories may reveal ⁽⁶⁾_____ evil things people do. For example, one story showed ⁽⁷⁾_____ way ⁽⁸⁾_____ man destroyed another man's family. Most soaps tell stories about love affairs. Finally, sometimes, ⁽⁹⁾_____ soap opera may teach ⁽¹⁰⁾_____ important lesson. This happened on ⁽¹¹⁾_____ soap opera when ⁽¹²⁾_____ young girl ran away from home. ⁽¹³⁾_____ program showed how running away did not solve her problems.

EXERCISE 9

Write five pairs of sentences using **a/an** for the first mention of a noun and **the** for the second mention of the noun.

Example: I read <u>an</u> interesting story in the newspaper. <u>The</u> story was relationships between men and women.

1. _____
2. _____
3. _____
4. _____
5. _____

EXERCISE 10

A. Write **a**, **an**, or **the** or an **X** if no article is necessary.

B. If you write X, explain why an article is not required.

1. What makes _____ hero? _____

2. Some say _____ heroes are born and not made. _____

3. This is true of many heroes in _____ classical literature. _____

4. They are born with _____ extraordinary abilities. _____

5. For example, _____ hero may have incredible strength. _____

6. He uses his strength as _____ weapon. _____

7. He fights _____ evil. _____

8. The evil thing may be _____ dragon or _____ person. _____

9. In _____ end, _____ heroes usually win. _____

10. In addition, some heroes have _____ knowledge of _____ world. _____

11. They use this knowledge to protect _____ land and people they love. _____

12. Some heroes build _____ bridge or _____ road. _____

13. Then they easily attack _____ enemy. _____

14. Also, heroes believe in _____ honor. _____

15. When they make _____ promise, they keep it. _____

16. They are loyal to _____ king or leader of their community. _____

17. _____ heroes will always carry out any orders they receive. _____

18. Sometimes _____ orders are dangerous. _____

19. For example, _____ hero can die trying to kill _____ dragon. _____

20. However, most heroes never think about _____ death. _____

21. Instead, _____ honor and loyalty make them brave. _____

EXERCISE 11

Knowing *when* to use an article is often just as difficult as knowing which article to use. In the following exercise, make a sentence from the scrambled lists of words given to you. Articles are *not* provided, so you must decide which article to use where. Check your punctuation and spelling. The first one is done as an example for you.

1. ESL students difficulty knowing articles have how use to language English in often

   ESL students often have difficulty knowing how to use the articles in the English language.

2. two are of definite there articles types indefinite and

3. include a the an definite and includes articles article indefinite

4. idiomatic of very use articles is

5. what this makes is so it hard

6. first whose Spanish students language Italian French have problems is don't have or others

7. characteristics have of languages as more same language these English

8. problems if student has with listening articles radio help will to

9. remember mastery student long also should that of takes time language

10. practice to in perfection key is language learning

EXERCISE 12

Write **a**, **an**, or **the** or write an **X** if no article is necessary.

Do situations also make (1)_____ heroes? (2)_____ situation made (3)_____ hero of my friend's son. My friend and her family had recently moved to (4)_____ lovely neighborhood in Georgia. Many families lived on (5)_____ street. Everyone was friendly and kind. One day, (6)_____ two-year-old neighbor found (7)_____ unlocked door. She opened it quietly and went outside to play. She played with (8)_____ toys in (9)_____ backyard. Her parents thought she was in her room. After (10)_____ few minutes, she became bored. She walked down to (11)_____ small pond behind her house. She looked at (12)_____ houses all around (13)_____ pond. Then she walked into (14)_____ water. She picked up some leaves that were floating on (15)_____ water. She reached for (16)_____ large leaf and fell on her face. She kicked and splashed but could not get up. (17)_____ little girl could not call for her mother.

My friend lived in (18)_____ house next door. Her fifteen-year-old son, Rafael, was working on (19)_____ school project. It was (20)_____ time for (21)_____ break. He decided to go fishing in (22)_____ pond out back. As Rafael walked toward (23)_____ pond, he saw something white in (24)_____ water. He ran quickly to (25)_____ pond and pulled (26)_____ little girl out of (27)_____ water. He screamed, "Mom! Dad! Help! Help!" (28)_____ noise brought his family and (29)_____ neighbors outside. They found him performing (30)_____ C.P.R. My friend called (31)_____ 911. Rafael acted quickly in this emergency situation and saved (32)_____ little girl's life. (33)_____ local newspaper wrote (34)_____ article about Rafael. He will always be (35)_____ hero.

EXERCISE 13

A. Write **a**, **an**, or **the** or write an **X** if no article is necessary.

My friend, Monica, also became (1)_____ hero. Monica loves to go to (2)_____ beach during her vacation. She works hard as (3)_____ nurse in (4)_____ Chicago hospital, so sometimes she needs to take (5)_____ break. Last year, Monica went to (6)_____ beach in Florida during her vacation. She stayed at (7)_____ hotel right on (8)_____ beach. She enjoyed swimming in (9)_____ water and walking on (10)_____ beach. Monica enjoyed being away from (11)_____ emergency room for (12)_____ few days.

One afternoon, Monica was sitting in her chair in (13)_____ sand. Lots of people were in (14)_____ water. Many others were sitting on (15)_____ beach towels or in (16)_____ chairs. Suddenly, (17)_____ blue sky became dark. Big storm clouds surprised everyone on (18)_____ beach. Rain fell hard. People looked for (19)_____ protection. Some ran to (20)_____ hotel down (21)_____ beach. Others ran to their cars in (22)_____ parking lot. Monica seemed frozen in her chair. She saw (23)_____ teenage girl leave (24)_____ water. Monica stood up and turned. She saw (25)____ girl run toward (26)_____ parking lot. Then the teen slipped and fell on (27)_____ pavement and did not get up. Monica ran to help (28)_____ girl. She found her lying on (29)_____ ground, unconscious. Monica screamed for (30)_____ help. Four people came running. Monica asked them to create (31)_____ protective cover over (32)_____ girl with their bodies and towels. One of them had (33)_____ cell phone and called (34)_____ 911. Monica used her nursing skills to assess (35)_____ injury and revive (36)_____ unconscious girl. When (37)_____ paramedics arrived, they said Monica was (38)_____ hero. (39)_____ teenager and her parents sent Monica (40)_____ huge bouquet of flowers with a card that said, "Thanks, Hero!"

21

1. Choose a piece of your own writing, a paragraph in length or longer, that you can edit for correct article usage.

2. Underline each noun.

3. Examine each noun, asking the following questions to determine if you need to change your use of articles:

   ◆ Is the word a count or noncount noun? Remember that you don't generally need to use an article with a noncount noun.

   ◆ Is the noun a proper noun, abstract noun, or gerund? If so, you probably do not need to use an article.

   ◆ Is this the first mention of the noun? Or is the noun referring to something specific? Should you use "the" with the noun?

4. Finally, make note of any questions you have about your article usage to ask a teacher.

PART III

VERBS

Verbs are words that show action or link the subject to the rest of the sentence. **Verbs** also indicate the time the action took place, for example, present, past, or future. A sentence must have a noun and a verb, therefore, a verb is a key element in a sentence. Here are some rules to help you choose correct verbs.

- Change the form of the **verb** according to person and tense (see Chapter 3):

  I run around the track five times every day.   (1st person singular; present tense)

  Joe talks about joining me.   (3rd person singular; present tense)

  Joe and Nick studied the effects of jogging.   (3rd person plural; past tense)

  Mary and Richard will get married tomorrow.   (3rd person plural; future tense)

- Use the correct regular and irregular forms of past tense verbs:

  Regular verbs add -d or -ed: walk, walked   dry, dried   arrive, arrived

  Irregular verbs may or may not have a different spelling: give, gave   hit, hit   strike, struck

- Never use the basic form of a verb after any form of the helping verb *to be*—is, are, was, were, be, being, been. Instead, use an –ing form of the verb (see Chapter 4):

  Correct: Yes, Mr. Smith is working late. or Yes, Mr. Smith works late.

  Incorrect: Yes, Mr. Smith is work late. (The main verb, *work*, needs -ing.)

- In negatives and past tense, helping verbs change form while action verbs stay in basic form:

  Correct: Alicia doesn't have any money today.

  Incorrect: Alicia doesn't has any money today. (The main verb, *has*, should be in the basic form.)

- Verbs in infinitive verb phrases are always written in basic form following the word *to*: to wish, to eat, to hope (see Chapter 6).

Example: We're going to eat dinner at six o'clock.

CHAPTER 3

Tenses

PRESENT TENSE

Present tense is used for habitual or repeated actions, actions taking place in the present time and to show custom and habit.

> My parents always **eat** breakfast. (custom)
>
> I **take** a pottery class on Wednesdays. (repeated actions)
>
> I **want** the brown shoes, please. (present time)
>
> I **wear** brown shoes with my tweed suit. (habitual action)

PAST TENSE

Past tense is used for actions begun and completed in the past. They are often indicated by a time word.

> I **moved** four times last year.
>
> Several years ago, I **took** violin lessons.
>
> Last night, there **was** nothing on television but reruns.

FUTURE TENSE

Future tense is used to express actions and being that will take place in the future. It is formed in one of two ways: (1) using the modal auxiliary "will" and the infinitive form of the main verb, and (2) using the appropriate form of be with the "going to" expression and the infinitive form of the main verb.

> She **will call** her parents when she returns from the retreat.
>
> They **are going to be** here soon, aren't they?
>
> I **won't** have time for breakfast today because I'm late.
>
> You're **going to be** sorry for that someday.

PRESENT PERFECT TENSE

Present perfect tense is used to indicate an action that began in the past but continues into the present and the expectation is that it will continue into the future.

> I **have lived** in this state for five years. (I moved here five years ago. I live here now. I expect to continue living here.)
>
> She **has been** an emergency room nurse since she graduated from nursing school. (She started as a nurse in the emergency room in the past. She is now a nurse there. We expect she will be in the future.)

PAST PERFECT TENSE

Past perfect tense indicates an action that occurred before another action in the past. We most often use two verbs in the sentence, one in the past and the other in past perfect tense.

John **had cooked** dinner before I finished my homework. (His action occurred before mine.)

FUTURE PERFECT TENSE

Future perfect tense refers to an action that, while not finished or accomplished now, will be finished or accomplished at some set time in the future.

They **will have learned** of their test results before they leave school today.

I **will have been married** ten years next week.

Note: This tense is most often combined with the present tense of another verb, not with the future tense.

Incorrect: He will have been home two hours before I will arrive.

Correct: He will have been home two hours when I arrive.

CONTINUOUS OR PROGRESSIVE TENSES

All of these tenses also have a "progressive" or "continuous" form. The present continuous tense is formed by using the appropriate form of be + the -ing form of the infinitive verb. The be form is called the *helping verb*. The present continuous tense strongly emphasizes an action taking place right now.

I **am talking** on the phone right now, so please do not interrupt me.

They **are waiting** for the bus in the pouring rain. (Raining and waiting now)

That noise **is driving** me crazy. (Right now)

They **are thinking** about having a family. (It's a topic of conversation over and over again right now in the present.)

He **is using** the Internet a lot more lately.

My parents **are worrying** themselves to death over their debts.

The past continuous tense is often, although not always, combined with another past tense. It indicates an action that was continuing during a time in the past.

They **were trying** to escape from prison when they got caught.

During the Vietnam War, many college students **were marching** in protest.

I'm sorry! **Were you sleeping**?

They **were frying** potatoes when the smoke alarm sounded.

The present perfect continuous tense is formed with the appropriate form of have + been + the -ing form of the infinitive verb. It is used to emphasize the continuity of a verb in the present perfect tense and is often used in conjunction with a verb in past tense.

> I **have been having** terrible nightmares lately. (Emphasis)
>
> She **has been taking** Spanish since the tenth grade. (She hasn't had one year of school since tenth grade when she didn't take Spanish.)
>
> They **have been writing** to each other since they became pen pals in 1998. (Notice the combination of present perfect continuous with past tense.)

The past continuous tense is formed by adding had + been + the -ing form of the infinitive verb. It emphasizes the continuity of an action in the past and is often combined with past tense or used alone.

> They **had been driving** an old Volvo until last year when they bought a Suburu.
>
> She **had been caring** for that elderly couple for five years. (It's implied that she is not now caring for them; either they have died or she has moved on or they've hired someone else.)

The future continuous tense is not common. It implies a stopping point, also in the future. It is formed with will + have/has + been + the -ing form of an infinitive verb.

> I **will have been wearing** soft contact lenses for five years this September. (What is the difference here from, "I have been wearing contacts for five years"? Not too much is different except the addition of "this September," which is the stopping point in the future.)
>
> The students **will have been studying** for ten hours by tomorrow morning.
>
> The pilot **will have been flying** the plane for ten hours by the time we arrive in Rome. (Right now, the flight is beginning or at least it is not finished. The tense then implies a projection into the future.)

EXERCISE 14

Complete the following sentences, describing what your routine is each day. Use present tense verbs in each sentence.

1. Every morning I _____

2. After that I _____

3. I always _____

4. I never _____

5. In the afternoon I usually _____

6. In the evening I _____

7. Before I go to bed I always _____

EXERCISE 15

A. Underline the correct present tense verb.

B. Change all the underlined verbs to past tense and add an appropriate time phrase where needed.

Example: We (<u>visit</u>, visits) a different city every summer.

   We visited a different city last year.

1. Our plane (land, lands) in Austin, Texas.

   _____

2. Austin (are, is) hot but beautiful in the summer.

   _____

3. Flowers (bloom, blooms) on many plants.

   _____

4. We (rent, rents) a van at the airport.

   _____

5. My husband (drive, drives) us to our hotel.

   _____

6. Everyone (get, gets) out quickly.

   _____

7. I (bump, bumps) my head on the doorway of the van.

   _____

8. My husband and children (walk, walks) into the hotel ahead of me.

   _____

9. The bellman (bring, brings) me some ice for my head.

   _____

10. I (tell, tells) him, "I (have, has) a headache!"

   _____

11. We all (laugh, laughs).

   _____

12. There (are, is) a waterfall and many plants in the lobby.

   _____

13. The hotel (have, has) a lovely dining area.

_____

14. Our suite (seem, seems) pleasant and comfortable.

_____

15. From the window, I (see, sees) the river.

_____

16. My husband (unpack, unpacks) our suitcases.

_____

17. The children (go, goes) for a walk to find some ice.

_____

18. I (look, looks) over the brochures and (begin, begins) planning our adventures.

_____

19. We (decide, decides) to visit the University of Texas first.

_____

20. The Gutenberg Bible (are, is) in the university's library.

_____

21. We (stand, stands) quietly in front of the old book.

_____

22. Then the children (walk, walks) around the museum by themselves.

_____

23. My husband and I (spend, spends) some time looking at paintings.

_____

24. Later, the family (meet, meets) and (drive, drives) to another museum.

_____

25. This museum (display, displays) works by Georgia O'Keeffe and other southwestern artists.

_____

26. The paintings of Indians (fascinate, fascinates) the children.

_____

27. I (love, loves) O'Keeffe's large flower paintings.

_____

28. My husband (prefer, prefers) the drawing of the sand dunes.

_____

29. The gift shop (contain, contains) many unique items.

_____

30. We (buy, buys) the book with all the artwork in this special exhibit.

_____

31. The next day, we (decide, decides) to drive out to see former President Lyndon B. Johnson's home.

_____

32. Acres of plants and flowers (cover, covers) the ground around the home.

_____

33. Rocking chairs still (sit, sits) on the porch.

_____

34. The children (recall, recalls) their recent history lessons on Johnson's presidency.

_____

35. We (like, likes) visiting places with special significance.

_____

36. On the way back to Austin, we (stop, stops) at a restaurant.

_____

37. The restaurant (are, is) located in Hill Country overlooking a beautiful lake.

_____

38. The name of the restaurant (represent, represents) what we (need, needs)—The Oasis.

_____

39. We (are, is) hot and thirsty from the warm Texas air.

_____

40. This lovely place (offer, offers) us an hour of relaxation and good food.

_____

41. Salsa and chips (arrive, arrives) as soon as we (sit, sits) down.

_____

42. Soon, our cool drinks (appear, appears).

_____

43. After a delicious meal, we (head, heads) back to the hotel.

_____

EXERCISE 16

A. Write the correct form of the verb in parentheses for each sentence. In addition, answer the questions about when we use the present tense and the present progressive tense:

1. He (like) _____ to play soccer.

2. I (work) _____ until 5 o'clock every day.

3. Answer the following question: When should we use the simple present tense?

4. I (take) _____ a test right now.

5. She (enjoy) _____ the book that she (read) _____.

6. Answer the following question: When should we use the present progressive tense?

B. Complete the following paragraph by inserting the correct form of the verb in parentheses:

Right now, I [7] (work) _____ at a restaurant as a waitress. I really [8] (like) _____ my job because I [9] (meet) _____ a lot of interesting people. There is a man at the table I [10] (serve) _____ right now who just returned from a trip to Paris. He [11] (work) _____ for a company that asks him to travel a lot. Perhaps his job is even more interesting than mine!

EXERCISE 17

Write the correct simple past tense form of the verb provided.

Example: Rafael (decide) <u>decided</u> to quit his job.

1. He (have) _____ to choose a new line of work.

2. Working at the automobile factory (be) _____ difficult.

3. Rafael (hate) _____ the long hours and low pay.

4. He (want) _____ a career.

5. His communication skills (be) _____ excellent.

6. He (go) _____ to work after high school.

7. His wife (tell) _____ him to consider college.

8. Going to college (seem) _____ so difficult. Who would pay?

9. Rafael and his wife (visit) _____ the local community college.

10. The counselor (explain) _____ the various scholarship and loan programs.

11. Fortunately, Rafael (qualify) _____ for two scholarships and a loan.

12. His wife (encourage) _____ him to study full time.

13. The college (offer) _____ a career inventory test on Saturdays.

14. Rafael (take) _____ the test.

15. He (discover) _____ skills in marketing, sales, and other business areas.

EXERCISE 18

Write the correct simple past tense form of the verb provided.

Signing up for classes (1)(be) _____ not easy. Rafael (2)(be) _____ older than most typical students. He (3)(begin) _____ to worry about his ability. Could he do well? Finally, he (4)(choose) _____ four classes. He (5)(sign) _____ up for English, humanities, science, and math. These (6)(be) _____ subjects he (7)(enjoy) _____ in high school ten years earlier. Arriving at the classroom early, Rafael (8)(notice) _____ many older students. Well, he (9)(think) _____ to himself, going to college might be okay. He (10)(introduce) _____ himself to three classmates. Two (11)(be) _____ his age; one (12)(be) _____ younger. They quickly (13)(become) _____ friends and (14)(study) _____ together.

Rafael and his new friends (15)(decide) _____ to prepare for the math final exam together. They (16)(meet) _____ at the college learning support center. When they (17)(have) _____ a difficult problem, they (18)(ask) _____ a tutor for help. The tutor carefully (19)(explain) _____ how to solve the problem. They (20)(repeat) _____ the process until they (21)(be) _____ ready for the test. All three of them (22)(receive) _____ A's or B's on the exam. Studying together (23)(give) _____ them encouragement. It also (24)(make) _____ them aware of their friendship..

EXERCISE 19

Answer the following questions by using the past tense.

1. Where did you live when you were young?

_____

2. Where did you go to school to learn English?

_____

3. What did your parents tell you to do when you were young?

_____

4. What was your favorite sport to play or watch when you were young?

_____

5. What was your favorite thing to do in your spare time when you were young?

_____

6. Where did you go on your favorite trip?

_____

7. What was the first thing you did when you woke up this morning?

_____

8. What was the best movie that you ever saw?

_____

9. What was the best book that you ever read?

_____

10. Who was the best friend that you ever had?

_____

EXERCISE 20

Choose one of the following prompts and write a short paragraph in the past tense.

• One day I was worried about a good friend when...

• One day I got lost and...

• The first time I spoke to someone in English was...

• My best friend did something nice for me one day when...

• I forgot an important appointment one day and...

_____

_____

_____

_____

_____

_____

_____

EXERCISE 21

A. The **subject** is set in bold. Underline the complete verb.

Examples: **Mr. Bruce** has been building homes for twenty-five years.

Mr. Bruce started building homes 25 years ago and continues until now.

1. **He** built the first home for himself.

_____

2. **His friends** thought **it** was lovely.

_____

3. **They** suggested, "**You** should build more homes."

_____

4. **Mr. Bruce** had recently retired from a career in the Air Force.

_____

5. **Sitting by the pool** was not for him.

_____

6. **He** was young and healthy.

_____

7. **He** had recently remarried.

_____

8. **His bride** agreed with their friends.

_____

9. **She** encouraged him to build another home.

_____

10. Thus, **his company** began.

_____

11. **It** continued to grow.

_____

12. **The company** built a home for Mr. Bruce's mother and stepfather.

_____

13. **They** loved the floor plans.

_____

14. **Mr. Stone**, his stepfather, watched the men build the house.

_____

15. **He** asked a lot of questions.

_____

16. **The workmen** were tired of answering his questions.

_____

17. **They** continued working when **he** visited the job site.

_____

18. **Mr. Bruce** answered his stepfather's questions.

_____

19. Soon **the house** was finished.

_____

20. **Mr. and Mrs. Stone** moved in and enjoyed their new home.

_____

B. Study the sentences using the past perfect tense and write a statement that shows your understanding of the use of the past perfect tense.

_____

_____

_____

_____

EXERCISE 22

A. The subject is set in **bold**. Underline the complete verb.

Building a new home requires patience and planning. First, **the builder** must draw the floor plans. **They** have to be exact. **The measurements** must be perfect. Sometimes, **the home buyer** may ask for changes in the plans. Then **the builder** must make appropriate changes to satisfy the buyer. **Builders** always want satisfied customers. After **the plans** are finished, **the builder** applies for the building permits. **These permits** establish the laws **the builder** must follow. Soon, the **construction crew** prepares the property. Then **the crew** lays the concrete foundation. **The builder** must make sure **the workers** do everything correctly. **The house** must pass all the inspections. **The right amount of materials** must be ordered. When **the materials** arrive, **they** must be carefully inspected. **Overseeing such a project** can be a rewarding experience.

Mr. Bruce enjoys the home-building process. After **the lumber** arrives, **he** guides the construction crew in putting up the frame of the house. Although **the walls** are not complete at this stage, **Mr. Bruce** can see in his mind what **the house** will look like. Usually, **he** is pleased with everything. **The house** begins to take shape when **the roof** goes on. Later, **the drywall** defines each room. Now **the structure** really begins to look like a house. During the construction process, **the new homeowners** select the colors and materials for the walls, floors, counters, and other areas. **They** get so excited thinking about their new home. **This** makes **Mr. Bruce** feel good, too. At last, **the house** is finished. **The landscape artist** plants grass, trees, shrubs, and flowers. What a pleasure **it** is for Mr. Bruce to see **the family** move into a new home. Now it is time to supervise the other houses **his crews** are working on. **Building homes** keeps Mr. Bruce mentally and physically active. **He** will never retire. **Life** is exciting when **he** keeps busy.

B. Rewrite this paragraph in past tense as follows: "**Building our new home** required patience and planning." Change all verbs to an appropriate tense, either past, present perfect, or past perfect. Underline the verbs you change.

_____

_____

_____

_____

_____

_____

_____

_____

_____

_____

C. Rewrite the first paragraph again, this time using the future tense. "**Building a new home** will require patience and planning."

_____

_____

_____

_____

_____

_____

_____

_____

_____

_____

EXERCISE 23

Write the correct form of the verb to be.

Example: Which season of the year <u>is</u> your favorite?

1. I can't decide which _____ my favorite.

2. Sometimes spring _____ the best time of year.

3. The flowers _____ in bloom.

4. The birds sing. They _____ happy as they build their nests.

5. During the spring, I _____ filled with a desire to _____ outside.

6. I go for a walk even if it _____ raining.

7. The rain smells fresh. It _____ clean and rejuvenating.

8. When I _____ in high school years ago, I preferred the winter.

9. We lived in Pennsylvania. It _____ cold there every winter.

10. My brothers and I loved the cold weather. We _____ happy when it snowed.

11. We went skiing on nearby hills. My brothers _____ excellent skiers.

12. I _____ not as proficient, but I loved it anyway.

13. I preferred ice skating. Skating _____ easier for me.

14. I recently went skating. I had not _____ on the ice in years.

15. I recalled all the winters in Pennsylvania. I _____ able to skate around and around and not fall.

16. It _____ hard to choose the best season.

17. Perhaps it depends on where we live and how old we _____ .

EXERCISE 24

Write a sentence or two in the future tense in response to the following questions:

1. What will you be doing at this time next month?

_____

_____

2. What will you be doing in five years?

_____

_____

3. Where are you going to go this weekend?

_____

_____

4. What will you do when you finish your English class?

_____

_____

5. When will you visit a good friend or family member next?

_____

_____

EXERCISE 25

Respond to each of the following questions by writing a complete sentence that uses the present perfect tense.

1. Have you been studying English for a long time?

_____

_____

2. How long have you been in school in the United States?

_____

_____

3. What kinds of jobs have you worked in the past?

_____

_____

4. Have you ever been sick and missed school?

_____

_____

5. Have you ever received an award or honor at school?

_____

_____

CHAPTER 4
Words with -ING:
Gerunds versus Continuous Verbs

Continuous/progressive tenses use the -ing form of a verb. But they aren't the only verbs that end in -ing. Gerunds are nouns formed by using verb + -ing. Usually you will use the gerund as the subject of the clause or as the object of some verbs and prepositions. Continuous verbs are formed the same way as gerunds, verb + -ing, but function as verbs. Continuous verbs are used with a form of the verb *to be*. Here are some examples to help you see the difference:

Gerunds as subjects (Remember, they are nouns now):

Shopping is Cathy's favorite thing to do.

Working late helps Cathy earn more money to spend in the stores.

Gerunds as objects:

Jim avoided hitting the car that moved into his lane.

He talked about buying a new truck with better brakes.

Contrast gerunds with continuous verb forms:

Alicia <u>is</u> working on her paper today.

Alicia <u>was</u> working on her paper yesterday.

She <u>was</u> trying to get it finished early. (She has been working on one paper or another all week.)

- Avoid fragments with gerunds and progressive verbs:

Correct:	Playing tennis in college was my dream.
	I was hoping to get a scholarship.
Incorrect:	Playing tennis in college. (The sentence is missing the verb and complete idea.)
	I hoping to get a scholarship. (The sentence is missing a form of the verb *to be*.)

EXERCISE 26

First, underline the gerunds and progressive verbs. Then write **G** on the line if the word is used as a gerund. Write **P** on the line if it is a progressive verb. If a form of the verb *be* is used with the -ing word, it is a progressive verb. Note the location of the verb *is* in the following two examples.

Examples: G   Shopping is Linda's favorite activity.

    P   When she is shopping, she feels happy.

_____ 1. Linda loves spending money.

_____ 2. Working late helps her earn extra money.

_____ 3. Recently, she was looking for a birthday present for her husband.

_____ 4. She was hoping to find a handsome watch.

_____ 5. Talking to the salesman was difficult.

_____ 6. He was helping three customers at the same time.

_____ 7. Linda was reaching in the case for a watch.

_____ 8. Suddenly, the salesman was running toward her.

_____ 9. Grabbing her hand, he said, "Stop."

_____ 10. "What are you doing?" he asked Linda.

_____ 11. She replied, "I'm looking at that watch."

_____ 12. Looking her in the eye, he said, "That's not possible."

_____ 13. Linda was getting angry.

_____ 14. Why was the salesman acting this way?

_____ 15. Was she going to stay or leave the store?

_____ 16. Was he going to show her the watch?

_____ 17. He was looking around the store at the other customers.

_____ 18. Finally, she asked, "Are you going to show me that watch?"

_____ 19. After all, selling watches was his job.

_____ 20. Smiling at her, he replied.

_____ 21. "Miss, selling those expensive watches is my job."

_____ 22. "Are you going to be able to pay for one?" he asked.

_____ 23. Smiling at the man, she said, "Of course."

_____ 24. Working long hours gave her plenty of extra money.

_____ 25. He was carefully taking the watch out of the case.

_____ 26. The watch was shining in the light.

_____ 27. Linda was beginning to feel happy again.

_____ 28. Shopping was so much fun.

_____ 29. The salesman was placing the watch in her hand so gently.

_____ 30. Turning over the price tag, Linda screamed, "$20,000!"

_____ 31. Finally, Linda was quiet, understanding the salesman's concern.

_____ 32. As Linda was handing the watch back to the man, she shook her head.

_____ 33. "Spending $20,000 on a watch is impossible for me," she said.

_____ 34. "I'm looking for one for about $200," she exclaimed.

_____ 35. This adventure was going to make a good birthday story.

EXERCISE 27

Underline the gerunds and progressive verbs. Then write **G** above the word if it is used as a gerund. Write **P** above the word if it is a progressive verb.

               G   **P**

Example: Studying is a full-time job. Phoning is studying for a math test.

Studying is a full-time activity when students are in college. Students will be spending time on course work both in and out of class. In class, students are going to take notes, answer questions, and ask questions. Participating in class helps students master the material. For example, answering the questions reinforces the instructor's lesson. In a science lab, carrying out the experiments teaches the students to use their knowledge in practical ways. However, keeping the mind focused in a lecture class is sometimes difficult. With so many things happening in their lives, students are finding it easy to let their minds wander. Students are trying to remind themselves to stay focused on the subject of the class. They know they are going to be more successful if they participate.

EXERCISE 28

A. Underline the gerunds and progressive verbs. Then write **G** above the word if it is used as a gerund. Write **P** above the word if it is a progressive verb.

         G   **P**

Example: Studying at home requires discipline. Akos was working on his homework until late.

B. Circle all helping verbs in the paragraph.

Students are finding they must spend a lot of time on their assignments at home. Many students will spend at least three hours on homework for every hour they were sitting in class that day. If a student is taking fifteen credits, that means he or she may spend about 45 hours on homework during the week. Memorizing formulas and getting math homework done can easily take nine hours a week. Writing a history research paper may take even more than nine hours a week. Of course, some courses are not going to require as much homework, especially if the student is proficient in the subject. For example, Felix is taking a computer class and is making A's; he studies only three hours a week. Basically, though, getting good grades in college depends on how much time students spend on homework.

C. Use the following words in two sentences, first as a gerund, and second as a part of a continuous (progressive) verb phrase.

Example: Studying is something most students avoid.

    I have been **studying** for my biology test for hours.

Voting

_____

_____

Standing

_____

_____

Doing

_____

_____

Improving

_____

_____

Rocking

_____

_____

Going

_____

_____

CHAPTER 5
Participles

An -ing verb can be used as part of a verb phrase with the helping verb or it can be used as adjective. In parts 1 and 2 of this unit, we've seen -ing verbs used in continuous tenses and as nouns called gerunds. Here are some examples of these same words used now as adjectives; we call them **participles.**

The **pleasing** smell of baking bread filled the house. (The smell was pleasing. The bread was baking.)

Turning to get a better look, the man crashed his car into the wall. (The man was turning.)

Caution: The two major problems in using participles involve sentences exactly like these two examples. In choosing the correct adjective to modify a noun, how do we know when to use a participle correctly?

The room smelled of (baking/baked) bread.

Is the bread still baking in the oven? If so, it is **baking** bread. Is the bread out of the oven, finished baking? If so, it is **baked** bread.

The play at the community college was quite (disappointing/disappointed).

The people who saw the play were disappointed. The play was disappointing.

The room was painted a (pleased/pleasing) color.

The people who are admiring the room are pleased. The color is pleasing to them.

Another frequent error involves dangling and/or misplaced participles. This occurs when a participle lacks an antecedent or the participial phrase is written after the wrong antecedent. Consider the following:

Hurrying to catch the bus (participial phrase), the doors closed.

Who is hurrying to catch the bus? We don't get that information in this sentence, but we should. This is a dangling participle. The sentence should correctly be written as:

Hurrying to catch the bus, Lisa barely made it just as the doors closed.

Who is hurrying? Lisa is. The antecedent clarifies the sentence.

Incorrect: The soldier crossed the enemy's foxhole **carrying his gun and hand grenades**. (participial phrase)

Here, the soldier is not carrying anything; the foxhole is. The participial phrase "carrying his gun and hand grenades" has been misplaced after the word "foxhole."

Correct: Carrying his gun and hand grenades, the soldier crossed the enemy's foxhole.

EXERCISE 29

Underline the participles in the following sentences.

1. During the Christmas season, many pleasing smells encourage the Christmas spirit.

2. Filling homes with their one-of-a-kind scent, freshly cut pine trees lend the most enticing smell of this season.

3. In addition to the comforting scent of pine, there is the bracing quality of the cold air making our breath misty.

4. Even families that seldom cook spend never-ending hours in the kitchen where they are cooking the family's typical seasonal specialty.

5. With the invigorating cold, the mouth-watering smells, and the continuing customs, it's no wonder that Christmas is almost everyone's favorite holiday.

EXERCISE 30

A. Underline the participial phrase.

B. Read the following sentences and decide if the participial phrase is **dangling** or **misplaced**. If it is, move the phrase to where it belongs or add an antecedent. On the line before the number, write M for Misplaced, D for Dangling, or C for Correct. The first one is done for you as an example.

___D___ 1. Hoping to beat the traffic, the accident occurred.

Hoping to beat the traffic, the motorist caused an accident.

_____ 2. The accident blocked both lanes, stopping traffic in each directions.

_____

_____ 3. The police officers arrived on motorcycles driving fast with the sirens screaming.

_____

_____ 4. Honking horns and screaming at each other, the confusion escalated.

_____

_____ 5. One man got out of his car waving a gun.

_____

_____ 6. Diving for the floorboards, the other motorists attempted to make themselves invisible.

_____

_____ 7. Soon the police officers apprehended the armed man carefully approaching.

_____

_____ 8. The situation was now handled safely reaching a dangerous level.

_____

_____ 9. The perpetrator was led from his car wearing handcuffs.

_____

_____ 10. Rerouting traffic and soothing nerves, the job of the police officers continues.

_____

EXERCISE 31

Combine each group of sentences into one, making use of participial phrases and continuous (progressive) verb forms. The completed exercise should be written as a paragraph, but each of the units is one sentence. The first one is done as an example.

THE TANGO

The man is dancing.

The man is wearing a hat.

The man is wearing high-heeled shoes.

The man is wearing a dark suit.

The man is dancing with a woman.

She is wearing a slit skirt.

She is wearing net stockings.

The stockings are dark.

The man wearing a hat, high-heeled shoes, and a dark suit is dancing with a woman wearing a slit skirt and dark net stockings.

The dancing is close.

The dancing is romantic.

_____

_____

The man steps between the feet.

The feet belong to the woman.

The woman is curving a leg.

The leg is curving around the man's.

People watch the dancing couple.

The dancing couple is whirling.

The dancing couple is dipping.

The dancing couple is twirling.

The dancing couple is turning right.

The dancing couple is turning left.

The couple is dancing to music.

The music is sad.

The music is like crying.

The music comes from an instrument.

The instrument is a bandoneon.

The instrument is like an accordion.

The dance is going on now.

The dance has been going on for over a
     hundred years.

The dance is in Buenos Aires, Argentina.

The dance is known as the Tango.

The dance is very popular.

CHAPTER 6
Infinitives

Infinitives are verb phrases composed of to + the main form of the verb:

To give, to see, to be, to think, to grow, to encourage, to worry.

Infinitives can be used as the subject of sentences:

"To be or not to be" is the question asked by Shakespeare's Hamlet.

To ski well is the aim of many winter sport enthusiasts.

Infinitive verbs follow "how, when, why, and where" (question words not used in questions):

I know how to sew.

Infinitive forms are used after other verbs: want/need/like/love/try:

I want to be alone.

I like to travel during the summer.

She needs to call her parents.

They tried to give the money back.

Birds must love to fly.

Infinitive forms are not used after the verbs: feel, see, hear, smell:

For example, consider a bus and your perception of it: I saw the bus move. I heard the bus move. I felt the bus move. (not "to move")

Do not use an infinitive after "enjoy."

I enjoy watching (not "to watch") sports on TV.

Do not use the infinitive after modal auxiliaries.

I must try harder in math class. (not I must to try)

I can sell you my car at a discount. (not I can to sell)

I will come by for you at nine o'clock.

He could make a mistake easily.

They should not touch the blood barehanded.

Some languages use a "that" clause in place of the infinitive in English. If your first language is Spanish, Italian, or French, beware of this. It is incorrect in English.

Incorrect: He wants that I help him.

Correct: He wants me to help him.

EXERCISE 32

Underline the infinitive verb in the following sentences. The first one is done for you.

1. Not many students know how to study.

2. To study correctly, a student should have a special place to go: a desk, the library, another room, or even a closet.

3. It is important to clear the head in order to get into a mood to study.

4. To clear the head, a student should write down everything that's interfering, jotting notes on a piece of paper to be looked at later.

5. Next, a student needs to gather pens, pencils, erasers, dictionary, books, and all other materials before starting to study.

6. Once a student has a place, materials, and a clear head, s/he can begin to follow a study process.

7. First, the student needs to read the notes from class, and then s/he will want to check the assignment book.

8. To read the textbook, a student needs skills such as prereading, scanning, skimming, and highlighting.

9. A student needs to include a break or two in the study time.

10. The break may also be a chance for the student to reward himself/herself with some snacks or perhaps a few minutes of listening to music.

11. The student returns from the break refreshed and ready to learn more.

12. These study sessions need to be short but well planned.

13. These methods for studying provide a routine that, repeated, becomes an easy habit to follow.

EXERCISE 33

Fill in the blanks with the correct verb form. Some are infinitives; some are not.

Travel is not only enjoyable but also one of the best ways (1)_____ (learn). When

we travel, we (2)_____ (learn) not only how (3)_____ (speak) words in another

language but also ways (4)_____ (appreciate) another culture. (5)_____ (live)

in or (6)_____ (visit) another country is hard, but it is easy (7)_____ (enjoy)

the differences if we try (8)_____ (relax) and try not (9)_____ (worry). For

example, it may be difficult (10)_____ (understand) how (11)_____ (order)

food in a foreign language and also how (12)_____ (shop) for things we

(13)_____ (need). But with every mistake we make, we learn how

(14)_____ (do) it better next time. Although food and customs may seem foreign at

first, we soon learn (15)_____ (see) that there are more similarities between us

than there are differences. Another thing travel can (16)_____ (teach) us is how

(17)_____ (rely) on ourselves. Many times we (18)_____ (find) ourselves

(19)_____ (face) a difficult situation with no one (20)_____ (turn) to for help.

For instance, we have learned (21)_____ (use) money of a different country, and

we often have (22)_____ (make) a decision about it quickly. Not everyone will

(23)_____ (treat) us honestly, this is a time when we have (24)_____ (try)

(25)_____ (rely) on our own intellect and instinct. (26)_____ (travel) gives us a

chance (27)_____ (learn) as much about ourselves as the foreign culture.

CHAPTER 7
Idiomatic Verbs

Idiomatic verbs are made up of the infinitive verb plus a preposition. They are also called **phrasal verbs**. They can be problematic because very often the meaning of the combined verb and preposition is completely changed from the meaning of the verb alone. There is no rhyme or reason for their idiomatic meanings; the only thing to do is to practice them and memorize them. Some of the most useful are:

- be about to: to be on the point of doing something

  We are about to study math.

- be off: leave or go away

  We are off at 6 o'clock.

- be on to: find or discover

  Jason thought he could trick his mother, but she was on to him and his plot.

- be over: finished

  Since the worst of the storm is over, we can go back to our house.

- be up: happening

  What's up?

- be up to: doing

  What are you up to?

- break down: stop working

  My car broke down last Friday.

- break into: burglarize or enter without permission

  A thief broke into my friend's house last night.

- break off: stop, finish

  Sara broke off her relationship with her boyfriend of two years.

- break out: escape

  Some thieves broke out of the jail.

- break up: stop, finish

  The meeting broke up at ten o'clock.

- bring back: recall

  When I was looking at a couple in the disco, it brought back to me memories of my old boyfriend.

- bring in: earn

  My friend is going to bring in $500 per month.

- bring on: cause to happen

  The cat in the house brought on my allergy attack.

- bring up: educate, rear

  I'd like to bring my children up in a safe society.

- call off: cancel

  The English class was called off because the teacher had to travel.

- come across: discover

  I came across my lost pen in the pocket of my jeans.

- come back: return

  Ann is coming back from her trip next week.

- come into: inherit

  Kyle is going to come into a lot of money because of his father's death.

- come over/round: visit casually

  My friend told me to come over about nine o'clock for the study group.

- come up: be mentioned

  The boss spoke with me about my lateness, but my absence did not come up.

- come up with: originate

  John is always coming up with good ideas about saving money.

- get ahead: advance

  Tom is doing very well in his studies; he is sure to get ahead in his career.

- get away: escape

  Many prisoners got away from their guards yesterday.

- get back: return

  Since he had many appointments, he didn't get back until midnight.

- get down: depress

  My lack of motivation to diet and exercise regularly gets me down.

- get off: leave

  Katherine got off work early last night.

- get on: enter/board

  It is dangerous to get on the bus just as it is starting.

- get out: leave (vehicle)

  I decided to get out of the car the moment I saw my friend walking along the street.

- get over: recover

  The children got over their terrible colds, but they still cannot go back to school.

- get through: make contact (telephone)

  There was something wrong with the line, so I couldn't get through.

- get up: rise/stand

  I am accustomed to getting up early, and that's why I'm sleepy now.

  Gentlemen get up when a lady enters the room.

- give away: give for free

  Steve gave away the puppies since he could not sell them.

- give back: return

  My friends are not very good at giving back the books they borrow from me.

- give in: surrender

  I try to prevent my children from watching too much television, but I'm afraid I often give in.

- give out: distribute

  The teacher gave out the exams.

- give up: abandon/stop

  George gave up smoking on his doctor's advice.

- go ahead: lead the way

  You go ahead and ski down first.

- go around: be enough

  Children often fear that there is not enough love to go around in a family of many siblings.

- go away: leave

  I'm very angry at my friend because he went away.

- go back: return, retreat

  Mary is never going back to her friend's house.

- go by: pass

  Many years have gone by since I first saw the Empire State Building in New York City.

- go down: sink

  The *Titanic* went down almost a hundred years ago.

- go into: investigate

  Let's not go into that now; that topic makes me uncomfortable.

- go off: explode

  Police report that the bomb went off at midnight.

- go on: go ahead

  You go on without me, and I'll meet you at the restaurant.

- go on with: continue

  You must go on with college if you want a secure job in the future.

- go out: leave the house or have a date with someone

  Are you going out tonight? Do you and Sally go out every weekend?

- go over: re-examine, repeat.

  Once you finish the exam, you have to go over it to make sure you answered every question.

- go through: examine, review

  I have to go through my receipts before I file my income tax.

- go up: increase, rise

  New car prices are going up rapidly this year.

- make off with: steal

  When the thieves saw the police coming, they made off with the goods quickly.

- make out: to understand

  Because Lisa speaks with a very pronounced accent, I can't make out what she is saying.

- make up: invent or lie

  He always makes up lies, so I don't trust him.

- make up for: compensate for

  Since my boyfriend forgot my birthday, he has to make up for that mistake.

- put away: tidy up

  I have to put my things away before setting the table for dinner.

- put back: replace

  I put back the pencil I borrowed from you.

- put down: write

  The lawyer put down everything I said in the deposition.

- put in for: submit a proposal

  Terry put in for a raise, but her boss turned it down.

- put off: postpone

  The conference has been put off until next week.

- put on: dress

  I take off my clothes when I go to bed and put them on when I get up.

- put out: extinguish/get angry

  I put out the fire under the teapot before my friend had poured the water for his tea, so he was quite put out with me.

- put through: connect

  The telephone operator put me through almost immediately.

- put up: give someone a place to live

  It is so kind of you to put us up for the wedding.

- put up with: bear, tolerate

  I can't put up with slow drivers.

- rule out: eliminate something

  Luisa ruled out going to any English schools on the West Coast because it was too far away from her family.

- set back: delay (progress).

  Megan was making good progress in her ice skating, but a sprained ankle set her back several weeks.

- set off: start, leave

  My parents set off at dawn to catch their plane for Hawaii.

- take after: resemble

  Ken takes after his father; he was tall, blond, and funny too.

- take away: remove

  Club soda will take away a red wine stain.

- take back: return

  Tomorrow we have to take the books back to the library.

- take down: write

  The teacher took down the names of the students who had done their homework.

- take off: leave

  The plane took off at 11 o'clock.

- take out: remove or extract

  I have a terrible toothache, so I'll have to go to the dentist and have my tooth taken out.

- throw away: cast out

  I always hate to throw away pictures, even if they are old.

- throw out: reject

  The election officials had to throw out all the ballots.

- throw up: vomit

  Because she drank too much, she was throwing up in the bathroom.

- turn back: reverse direction

  The road was too muddy, so we had to turn back.

- turn down: refuse or reject

  The magazine turned down the poetry I submitted.

- turn into: become, change

  The worm turned into a butterfly in front of our eyes.

- turn off: switch off

  Turn off the lights before you go to bed.

- turn on: switch on

  She had a cup of coffee, and then she turned on the television.

- turn out: put out, extinguish

  Will you turn out the lights when you go to bed, please?

EXERCISE 34

1. Look at advertisements in an English language magazine or newspaper. Find as many of the idiomatic verbs listed here as you can.

2. Write down the sentence where the idiomatic verb is used.

_____

_____

3. Write your understanding of what the sentence means. Check your interpretations with a native English speaker or with your teacher.

_____

_____

_____

_____

1. Choose a piece of your own writing, a paragraph in length or longer, that you can edit for correct verb usage.

2. Underline the subject and circle the complete verb in each sentence.

3. Examine each verb, asking two questions: Does the verb agree with its subject? Is the verb tense correct for the meaning of the sentence?

PART IV

MODIFIERS

■ ■ ■

CHAPTER 8
Single Word Modifiers

Modifiers help clarify the meaning of nouns. Single-word modifiers may be just one word, like **some**, or may contain two or three words, like **a little** or **a lot of**. Notice the difference in meaning when different modifiers are added to the sentence, He needed money to buy a car.

With modifier: He needed <u>a lot of</u> money to buy a car.

With modifier: He needed <u>a little</u> money to buy a car.

Here are some rules to help you use modifiers:

- Precede singular count nouns with:

    this, that, other, another, one, any, every, each, neither, either, some

- Precede plural count nouns with:

    these, those, some, many, a lot of, few, a few, quite a few

- Precede noncount nouns with:

    much, any, some, a little, lots of, a lot of, this, that

- Use any to indicate a negative element, and use some to indicate certainty. Use either any or some for an uncertain idea:

    She <u>didn't</u> want any octopus, but she <u>did</u> eat some lobster.

    The others at the party <u>weren't sure</u> if they wanted any seafood.

    The others at the party <u>weren't sure</u> if they wanted some seafood.

- Use any in questions and negatives; some in affirmative statements. Example:

    Do you have any questions about grammar?

    No, I don't have any. I have some problems.

- Use other to mean "different." Use another to mean "additional."

    The other doctor was on vacation when the hospital decided to add another doctor to the case.

EXERCISE 35

A. Write **a few**, **a little**, or **any** in each blank.

B. Change the meaning of the sentence by writing **much**, **many**, **lots of**, **a lot of**, or **some** in the appropriate blanks.

1. The college cafeteria serves (quite) _____ students.

2. The cafeteria offers _____ choices for breakfast.

3. Some students eat _____ cereal for breakfast.

4. Others don't eat _____ cereal at all.

5. Only _____ students ask for eggs and bacon.

6. The cafeteria serves quite _____ glasses of orange and apple juice.

7. Many students drink _____ cups of coffee.

8. Some drink their coffee without _____ sugar or cream.

9. Students like to have _____ bagels with their coffee.

10. However, sometimes the cafeteria doesn't have _____ bagels.

11. Then the students have to eat _____ pieces of toast with butter and jelly.

12. They may have to eat _____ doughnuts in place of the bagels.

13. This makes the students feel _____ upset.

14. People who eat _____ doughnuts or pieces of toast every day might gain weight.

15. Then they may not want to eat _____ breakfast for awhile.

16. The cafeteria could lose _____ money if students do not eat breakfast.

EXERCISE 36

A. Write **a few**, **a little**, or **any** in the appropriate blank.

B. Write **much**, **many**, and **some** in the appropriate blank to change the meaning of the sentence.

The cafeteria's lunch is ⁽¹⁾_____ better than its breakfast. There are (quite) ⁽²⁾_____ more options. On the menu are ⁽³⁾_____ hot and cold meals. For example, students can choose a complete hot lunch with ⁽⁴⁾_____ vegetables and a main dish. Usually the cafeteria offers ⁽⁵⁾_____ choices for the main dish. Chicken, ground beef, or ham are popular, but some students prefer meals without ⁽⁶⁾_____ meat. Therefore, these students choose a vegetable dish because it doesn't contain ⁽⁷⁾_____ meat. Also on the menu are ⁽⁸⁾_____ other options such as hamburgers and hot turkey sandwiches with gravy. ⁽⁹⁾_____ students add ⁽¹⁰⁾_____ catsup or mustard to their hamburgers. ⁽¹¹⁾_____ French fries may complete the meal.

EXERCISE 37

A. Write **some** or **any** in the appropriate blank.

B. For each numbered statement, write a question that this statement could answer using **some** or **any**.

Example: Do students enjoy almost any activity . . . ?

1. After a long day, students enjoy almost _____ activity outside the class-room.

   _____

2. Eating is a favorite activity of _____ students.

   _____

3. Thus, _____ students enjoy dinner in the college cafeteria.

   _____

4. They will eat _____ food on their plates.

   _____

5. However, food is not the most important thing to _____ students.

   _____

6. _____ students go to the cafeteria to meet other students.

   _____

7. They enjoy _____ discussion about sports, fashion, or movies.

   _____

8. These students talk about _____ topic except food.

   _____

9. Sometimes they do not have _____ new ideas.

   _____

10. They continue to discuss _____ of the same old topics.

    _____

EXERCISE 38

A. Write **some** or **any** in the appropriate blank.

B. Change numbers 2, 5, and 8 to negative statements and then change some/any, accordingly.

(1)_____ day now the workers will complete their job. They are adding (2)_____ new rooms to the cafeteria. (3)_____ workers begin working before breakfast. However, we never see (4)_____ workers during lunch. They probably work on (5)_____ other project at that time. (6)_____ of the workers must take a lunch break; however, we never see (7)_____ of them eating in the cafeteria. They must have (8)_____ rules to follow. Perhaps one rule is (9)_____ worker who brings lunch must eat outside.

EXERCISE 39

A. Write **this** or **these** in the appropriate blank.

B. Change the nouns in sentences 1, 2, 6, and 7 to plural and use either **these** or **that**. Make other necessary changes to the sentences.

1. _____ nature program I'm watching is about wild and domestic animals.

2. Right now, _____ program is showing three domestic kittens.

3. _____ kittens are playing with pieces of string.

4. _____ pieces of string are each about two feet long.

5. The largest kitten wants _____ pieces of string for himself.

6. _____ type of activity also happens in nature.

7. The narrator explained _____ fact as the largest kitten attacked the others.

8. _____ is an interesting program.

EXERCISE 40

Write **this** or **these** in the appropriate blank.

Now the program is showing (1)_____ same behavior in lion cubs. This time (2)_____ animals are playing with long pieces of grass, not string. Once again, the largest one wants (3)_____ activity to become a fight. Such acts of aggression help determine which of (4)_____ lions will be the leader. All of (5)_____ lions look willing to fight. Humans are like (6)_____, too. The biggest one usually tries to dominate the others with (7)_____ same methods. Nature shows help us understand (8)_____ interesting facts about animals.

EXERCISE 41

A. Write **that/this** or **those/these** in the appropriate blank. Answers may vary although the answer given in the answer key will be the one that is the most natural sounding to native speakers.

B. For each sentence, explain why you made the choices you did in this exercise.

1. _____ movie about the famous ship, the *Titanic*, was realistic.

_____

2. First, the director made _____ characters seem real.

_____

3. _____ lovers belonged together.

_____

4. _____ type of love story interested everyone in my family.

_____

5. Second, _____ rooms looked like the ones in history books.

_____

6. Every detail in _____ elegant rooms was perfect.

_____

7. Last, _____ ending made us cry.

_____

8. We cried because _____ lovers could not be together.

_____

EXERCISE 42

Write **another**, **other**, or **others** in the appropriate blanks.

Some people prefer to read books about (1)_____ kinds of historical events. However, movies about (2)_____ subjects, are, often boring. For example, a movie in history class about the Civil War was (3)_____ kind of movie—boring. (4)_____ movie taught us about the war, but the narrator gave too many details. All (5)_____ facts put students to sleep. (6)_____ movie that is interesting is one made from a book. For example, *Robin Hood* is an interesting book and it made an interesting movie. (7)_____ are *Legends of the Fall*, *A River Runs Through It*, and *The Bridges of Madison County*. (8)_____ very powerful movie made from a book is *The Horse Whisperer*. There are many (9)_____ but no (10)_____ example is needed to prove that movies from books represent (11)_____ types of success in film.

CHAPTER 9
Adjectives and Adverbs

Adjectives and adverbs also modify words in the sentence. **Adjectives** describe or clarify nouns, pronouns, and groups of words that function as nouns. Usually, words that end in *-ful, -ness, -ish,* and *-less* are adjectives. Some common adjectives include beautiful, old, red, happy, useful, good. **Adverbs** describe or clarify verbs, adjectives, other adverbs, and entire sentences. Many adverbs end in *-ly,* but some have no special ending. Some common adverbs are usually, happily, therefore, well. Here are a few rules to help you master the use of adjectives and adverbs:

- In English, adjectives normally precede the nouns they modify.

  The tall, yellow flower grew in front of the old, unpainted garage door. Place adjectives near the nouns or pronouns to which they refer.

- Place adjectives near the nouns or pronouns to which they refer.

  The rich **woman** stepped into the elegant **limousine.**

  The **children,** tired and happy, ran into the house.

- Do not change the form of the adjective if the noun or pronoun is plural. Notice the adjectives, *happy* and *long,* do not become plural:

  The happy <u>students</u> sat around the long <u>tables</u> in the library.

- Put a list of descriptive adjectives in the following order: *judgment, physical characteristics, condition, composition,* and *origin* or *trade name:*

  The beautiful, tall, old, oak <u>tree</u> stood near the lake.

  The efficient, new, metal, Japanese <u>clock</u> works well.

- A comma is used between each of the adjectives used in a series. However, with only two or three adjectives preceding a noun, a comma is used if each of the adjectives separately modifies the noun. Deleting the comma changes the meaning of the sentence. Notice the difference in meaning for the following examples:

  A big, black bird stole my sandwich out of my hand in the Italian piazza! (The bird is big and also black, so we have a comma between big and black.)

  The dark red blood was hardly noticeable against the cowboy's black shirt. (In this sentence, the color red is dark. The word "dark" becomes a modifier of red, not of blood.)

- Sometimes an adverb can be moved to different locations in a sentence without changing the meaning. In the following two sentences, the meaning of quietly is the same:

Quietly, Mother **opened** the door to the baby's room.

Mother quietly **opened** the door to the baby's room.

- It is usually best not to separate an infinitive verb (to + verb) with an adverb. Many English instructors mark this split as an error called "split infinitive."

Incorrect: She asked me to carefully proofread my work.

Correct: She asked me to proofread my work carefully.

EXERCISE 43

A. Underline the adjective or adverb modifier. Draw a line to the word it modifies. There may be two modifiers for the same word. Do not underline *a, an,* or *the.*

B. Rewrite each sentence, using another modifier in place of the one you underlined. Use a synonym of the modifier so that the meaning of this exercise is not greatly changed.

C. Rewrite each sentence using the antonym, thereby changing the meaning of the sentence greatly.

Example: Many tourists take cruises to <u>foreign</u> countries. The cruise boat moves <u>gently</u>.

1. My grandmother took a long cruise in the South China Sea.

_____

_____

2. The cruise began in the modern port of Singapore.

_____

_____

3. The large white ship traveled across the sea to Vietnam.

_____

_____

4. Vietnam has 2,000 miles of interesting coastline.

_____

_____

5. Green rice paddies, or fields, are located along the coast.

_____

_____

6. People worked continuously in the rice paddies.

_____

_____

7. Some of them waved happily to the tourists on the cruise ship.

_____

_____

8. The cruise ship slowly sailed up the Saigon River.

_____

_____

9. There were many unusual things on the Saigon River.

_____

_____

10. Small fishing boats traveled quietly up the river.

_____

_____

11. Wooden houseboats also floated near the shore.

_____

_____

12. Entire families lived in the small space on the houseboats.

_____

_____

13. The boat people sold various items to the tourists on the ship.

_____

_____

14. The cruise ship traveled around old, large ships.

_____

_____

15. At Ho Chi Minh City, tourists left the cruise ship to take tours on smaller boats.

_____

_____

16. These boats moved quickly on the water.

_____

_____

EXERCISE 44

A. Underline the adjective or adverb that modifies the italicized word. There may be two modifiers for the same word.

B. Go back through the paragraph and change the modifier(s) to one of your own choice. Try not to change drastically the meaning of the paragraph with your changes.

The tour guide *talks* excitedly about Vietnam. He is a twenty-five-year-old man with a positive *attitude.* He is too *young* to remember the Vietnam War, or what he calls the American War. However, he enthusiastically *shows* the tourists some wartime sights. Then he takes them downtown to see wonderful *Ho Chi Minh City.* Many *shops* in Cholon (Chinatown) are 200 years old. The shopkeepers sell French bread, delicious *fruit,* straw *hats,* and colorful *clothing.* Businessmen and housewives excitedly *buy* different products. Nearby tall, new *buildings* stand. These hotels and office buildings clearly *show* the importance of commerce. Ho Chi Minh City is full of fascinating *contrasts.* The old and new happily *live* together.

EXERCISE 45

A. Underline the adjective or adverb that modifies the italicized word.

B. Add another modifier wherever there is only one. Pay special attention to the use of the comma.

The large cruise *ship* takes the passengers to other *areas* of Vietnam. The ship travels on the Perfume River, a gentle *body* of water. The calm *river* and lovely *sights* capture everyone's attention. The exotic *residence* of the emperor sits near the river. In the past, high *walls* provided necessary *protection* for many emperors. Unfortunately, some of the walls and buildings were totally *destroyed* during the war. However, the Vietnamese carefully *rebuilt* the library and the palace. The tombs of the emperors are located a short *distance* down the river. The lovely *tombs* look like small *palaces.* The emperor's residence and the tombs make this an important cultural *center.* The Vietnamese and foreign *tourists* pay their respects to these dead rulers.

EXERCISE 46

Underline the correct adjective or adverb.

(1)(Final, Finally), the winter holiday is here. My family will (2)(probable, probably) go to the mountains to ski. We love the (3)(beautiful, beautifully) scenery. We also love to ski. The tall, white mountains covered in snow provide (4)(many, more) opportunities for us to ski. We usually take the (5)(easy, easily) way up to the skiing area—we ride the ski lift. On a (6)(clear, clearly) day, the lift may even take us to the top of the tallest mountain. My brothers ski (7)(beautiful, beautifully), so I love to watch them go down the mountain. They (8)(easy, easily) pass between the trees. (9)(Clear, Clearly), they are better skiers than I am. I always fall (10)(many, more) times than they do. In the (11)(final, finally) analysis, though, we always have a wonderful time.

EXERCISE 47

Underline the correct form of the adjective or adverb.

Humanities students must attend cultural events or museums. I visited a museum and a library and saw a play. Some things were (1)(most interesting, more interesting) than others. For example, the art museum had (2)(beautiful, more beautiful) paintings than the old library. The library, though, had (3)(a better, the best) collection of books in the city. The librarian gave (4)(a better, the best) tour than the docent in the art museum. He told us (5)(many, much) details about the history of the town and the books. The museum docent took us through the museum (6)(much slowly, more slowly) than the librarian. Unfortunately, she didn't give us (7)(many, much) information. I liked the play (8)(better than, the best) the other activities. The actors wore (9)(the most, the more) beautiful costumes. The play was the (10)(most funny, funniest) I had ever seen.

EXERCISE 48

A. Fill in the missing adjective or adverb with a word from the list according to the information in parentheses. Make sure the meaning is clear. Use each word only once. Extra answers are provided. Answers may vary.

B. Write your own sentences correctly using each of the words.

Example: (Adv.) College students need to exercise regularly .

Adjective	Adverb
important	sometimes
tension	always
stressful	regularly
many	quickly
strong	easier
good	clearly
happy	frequently

1. (Adj.)   Exercising provides _____ benefits.

2. (Adj.)   First, exercising is _____ for the heart.

3. (Adj.)   A _____ heart works efficiently.

4. (Adv.)   Cells _____ need oxygen.

5. (Adj.)   Second, exercise helps relieve a _____ day.

6. (Adj.)   Students have so _____ pressures.

7. (Adv.)   They worry about school, work, and money which _____ causes headaches.

8. (Adv.)   Exercising can _____ eliminate those headaches.

9. (Adv.)   Finally, exercising can help students think more _____ .

10. (Adv.)   School assignments will be _____ to complete.

EXERCISE 49

Many nonnative speakers are tempted to believe that the key to learning a second language is learning more and more vocabulary. However, if you listen to the speech of children in any language, you will note that they communicate well with a limited vocabulary. You should not be too hard on yourself if your vocabulary in English seems small. Take advantage of every opportunity to learn and use new words. You should use a new word 10 times in the first day to make it part of your vocabulary. On this sheet of paper, below these instructions, make a list of the adjectives and adverbs you believe you most often use right now. Then write a new word that means the same and try to use it 10 times today. Do the same for all the new words you write. How do you find synonyms? (1) Go back through these modifier exercises and list words that are unfamiliar to you, (2) Look up the word you do use in a thesaurus to find its synonym.

Familiar adjective/adverb	Synonyms

If you have been working through this workbook in order, then you have studied nouns, verbs, adjectives, and adverbs. You might want to review the information in those parts of the book before completing this editing exercise.

1. Choose a piece of your own writing, a paragraph in length or longer, that you can edit for correct use of modifiers.

2. Underline the nouns in the piece of writing and circle the complete verbs.

3. Examine each underlined noun to see if modifiers are used correctly. Did you use the correct form of the word to modify the noun? Is the modifier placed in the correct location? If you use more than one modifier to modify the same noun, were you certain to use an adverb to modify an adjective?

4. Examine each circled verb to see if modifiers are used correctly. Did you use the correct form of the word to modify the verb? Is the modifier placed in the correct location? If you use more than one modifier to modify the same word, were you certain to use an adverb to modify an adjective?

PART V

PRONOUNS

CHAPTER 10
Object Pronouns

Pronouns replace nouns or noun phrases. We use pronouns frequently. The word the pronoun replaces is called the **antecedent.** The pronoun that refers to this antecedent is called the **referent.** Pronouns must agree with nouns in usage, gender, and number. Here is a list of pronouns:

	Subject		Object		Possessive		Reflexive (-self)	
Person	Sing.	Plural	Sing.	Plural	Sing.	Plural	Sing.	Plural
First	I	we	me	us	my/mine	our/ours	myself	ourselves
Second	you	you	you	you	your/yours	your/yours	yourself	yourselves
Third	he she it	they	him her it	them	his her/hers its	their/theirs	himself herself itself	themselves

- Avoid pronoun reference problems by making sure you know the exact antecedent the pronoun replaces. In the following sentences, the antecedents and pronouns are in bold type:

  The **mountains** near the town of San German, Puerto Rico, are beautiful. **They** are covered with many tropical plants.

  My **parents** bought a house near the mountains. **They** really liked the house.

  My **mother** said the house was perfect. **She** was glad to move out of town.

- Pronouns frequently function as subjects of sentences. Some languages do not always require a subject because the verb form indicates what the subject is. English does require that a subject be physically present. For this reason, in English we have something called "the dummy it." We use the pronoun "it" in the subject position of a sentence when there is no clear noun or pronoun to be used. For example, It is raining. (What is "it"? Who knows?) It is a "dummy" because it doesn't seem to mean anything. It is used simply as a place keeper because we have to have a subject for the sentence in English. We use this sentence construction to talk about the weather as well as other things.

It is cold. It is windy. It's hot in here.

It is never too late to learn in life.

It would be a miracle if I won the lottery.

} What "it" is isn't clear, but we must have a subject for the sentence.

It is wise to stay in bed and drink lots of fluids when you have a cold.

It is sad when someone wastes time.

It is expensive to fly to Argentina.

It is the elderly who suffer most from the cold.

Correct: **John** has some plans for tonight. **He** is going bowling.

Incorrect: **John** has some plans for tonight. Is going bowling. (The subject **He** is missing.)

Correct: Where is your **book**? Is **it** in the car?

Incorrect: Where is your **book**? Is in the car? (The subject **it** is missing.)

- Do not use the antecedent and the pronoun together. Use the pronoun or the noun.

Correct: **Erika's** hobby is horseback riding. **She** goes to the barn every day.

Incorrect: **Erika's** hobby is horseback riding. Erika ~~she~~ goes to the barn every day.

Pronouns can be one of the most frustrating grammatical concerns in the English language. Native and nonnative speakers alike share a difficulty in getting pronouns right in sentences. Here are a few clues to help you.

- Notice that subject pronouns belong in the subject position of a sentence. Sounds easy, but is it really? Notice that the subject positions are marked in bold in the following sentence.

Jack and Jill bought a new car for their parents, and **the parents** gave Jack and Jill a new refrigerator in return.

- Subjects of sentences in English usually precede the verbs in declarative sentences. So **Jack and Jill** are in the subject position. So are **the parents** since they are the subject of the second clause. In this case, there are no other subjects. To replace these subjects, then, we find the corresponding subject pronouns on the chart. In this case, "they" is used in both positions.

Jack and I bought a new car for our parents. (This is an example of the "domino effect" of pronouns in English: when one changes in a sentence, frequently they all change. Now Jack and I are the subjects, so the parents become "our" instead of "their.")

82

EXERCISE 50

A. Underline the correct subject pronoun.

B. Draw a line to the word(s) the pronoun refers to (its antecedent). Note that the antecedent may be in another sentence.

Example: Although my twins look alike, (they, he) have different personalities.

1. First, my son, Andre, is friendly. (He, She) talks to everyone.

2. Sometimes, (he, she) talks to people in line at the grocery store.

3. (He, They) respond to him in a friendly way.

4. On the other hand, my daughter, Aisha, is shy. (He, She) only talks to people if (he, she) knows them.

5. (He, She) loves to have long conversations with friends on the phone.

6. The twins are also different in the way (they, he) laugh.

7. Andre's laughter is big and loud. (He, She) wants everyone to laugh, too.

8. (He, She) loves to watch funny movies.

9. Aisha, though, laughs in a quiet way. (They, She) always puts her hand over her mouth.

10. The biggest difference is in the way (he, they) get angry.

11. Andre yells and screams. (They, He) jumps up and down.

12. I have to send him to the bedroom. Ten minutes later, (they, he) comes out laughing.

13. (She, He) cannot even remember why (she, he) was angry.

14. Aisha never yells. (They, She) just gets quiet.

15. I worry because (she, he) does not express her feelings.

16. (They, She) remembers everything; Andre remembers nothing.

17. Having twins provides many pleasures. (They, He) are wonderful children.

EXERCISE 51

Underline the correct subject pronoun.

My family and I went to the circus. [1](We, They) enjoyed every minute. My mother and aunts liked the mirrors in the Haunted House. [2](They, She) said the mirrors made them look small. My dad enjoyed the clowns. [3](He, They) laughed every time a clown drove a small car around the center ring. One clown with red gloves got out of the car. [4](He, They) came over to us. [5](He, They) shook my dad's hand. Dad laughed when [6](he, she) saw his red hand. My little brother said [7](he, she) liked the animals the best. [8](He, She) said the tigers did not scare him. However, [9](she, he) jumped when the tiger roared. I enjoyed the trapeze artists the best. [10](They, He) flew through the air so gracefully, and [11](she, they) always landed perfectly. The circus was so much fun!

EXERCISE 52

A. Underline the correct subject pronoun.

B. Above each subject pronoun, write the noun it refers to.

A father and his daughter perform for the audience. [1](He, They) are acrobats in a small circus. [2](She, He) lifts the small girl into the air. [3](She, He) puts three bowls on her head and stands so carefully in his hand. [4](She, They) slowly moves her right foot behind her head. How graceful [5](she, he) is! Next, [6](he, they) lifts her higher, so [7](she, he) can stand on his head. [8](She, He) puts her left foot out in front and almost sits on his head. The bowls never move. [9](They, It) remain on her head. [10](He, She) never looks up while his daughter is on his head. [11](They, He) both remain very still and continue smiling. Then [12](she, he) reaches down for her father's hand. [13](He, They) swings her around and up. Finally, [14](he, she) gently brings her to the ground. The audience applauds with enthusiasm as [15](she, they) removes the bowls from her head. Before [16](they, she) leave, [17](they, she) bow to the audience, and the young girl throws kisses.

EXERCISE 53

A. Write the missing subject pronoun in the blank.

B. Then draw a line to the noun(s) the subject pronoun refers to. Underline the noun or noun phrase. *Note:* In some cases, the referent may refer to an antecedent in a previous sentence.

Example: Mom and dad moved to Puerto Rico. They moved there in 1973.

1. My father studied at the University of Puerto Rico in Mayaguez. _____ studied in the Department of Marine Sciences.

2. Dad was an excellent student. _____ enjoyed every assignment.

3. Mom was a teacher. _____ taught in a small Catholic school in San German.

4. _____ taught English to students in the fifth through eighth grades.

5. When my mother moved to Puerto Rico, _____ could not speak much Spanish.

6. That was good for the students. _____ learned a lot of English.

7. Many students learned to speak English very well. _____ also took other classes in English.

8. In 1977, Dad graduated. _____ received a Ph.D. in marine sciences.

9. _____ applied for a job in the United States.

10. Unfortunately, _____ could not find a job in his field.

11. Finally, _____ applied for a job at the University of Puerto Rico.

12. Dad received the job offer. _____ was a good job.

13. _____ accepted the job.

14. Mom and Dad were happy. _____ liked living in Puerto Rico.

EXERCISE 54

Write the missing subject pronoun in the blank.

During the first five years Mom and Dad lived in Puerto Rico, (1)_____ traveled to some Caribbean islands. (2)_____ traveled to Haiti, the Dominican Republic, and the Virgin Islands. (3)_____ learned about the people in these countries. Mom felt sad because many of the people were poor. However, (4)_____ discovered that most people seemed happy. (5)_____ smiled and waved at her during her shopping trips. My parents also learned about the different languages. Dad understood the Spanish spoken in the Dominican Republic; however, (6)_____ could not understand the French or Creole spoken in Haiti. In St. Thomas, (7)_____ both had no trouble understanding the language. (8)_____ had many wonderful adventures in the Caribbean.

CHAPTER 11
Object/Possessive Pronouns

Object pronouns give students more trouble than subject or possessive or reflexive pronouns. The clue is to figure out what position the pronoun is in the sentence. The chart on page 81 is once again helpful. Pronouns in the object position in a sentence must come from those object pronouns, which are:

Singular	Plural
me	us
you	you
him/her	them

Notice the positions in each sentence below where object pronouns must be used. Those positions are further illustrated for you by the box.

The teacher asked (I/me) ⎢OBJ⎢ to give back the papers.

I wanted he/him ⎢OBJ⎢ to take Jim and (I/me) ⎢OBJ⎢ to the party.

Theresa rescued (they/<u>them</u>) and took (they/<u>them</u>) to (she/<u>her</u>).

So, the object positions in sentences are as follows:

Object of the preposition, as in

to + ⎢object⎢

for + ⎢object⎢

about + ⎢object⎢

in + ⎢object⎢

Example: Give it to John and to me.

- Please return your comments to the director and me. (Note: Many business people write, "Please return your comments to the director and myself. This is incorrect. Note that this is the reflexive, not the object pronoun, as it should be.)

- Object of the verb, as a direct object or indirect object.

Mr. Johnson delivered the card to Amy. Mr. Johnson delivered it to her.

Hint: Remember that it will always be *to them/to him/to her/to me/to us*. It will never be *to they/to she/to he/to we.*

EXERCISE 55

A. In each sentence, choose between the object or possessive pronoun. Underline the correct one.

B. At the end of each sentence, write a "P" for possessive if you used the possessive pronoun form or an "O" for object if you used the object form.

1. In the United States, people love football. Each football team has (its, it) own uniform.

2. Football players wear special uniforms to protect (their, them) from injury.

3. Players need special helmets to protect (their, them) heads.

4. The men on the field throw (their, them) bodies on top of other players.

5. A player can easily get hurt in (his, him) neck or head.

6. (Their, Them) helmets also have special mouthpieces.

7. The players bite down on (their, them).

8. This helps (their, them) keep (their, them) teeth.

9. Football players also wear special pads on (their, them) shoulders.

10. These pads absorb pressure. A player can push (his, him) shoulder into an opponent.

11. Unfortunately, the uniform does not always prevent injury. In a game I saw, a player lost (his, him) helmet.

12. He didn't get up. (His, Him) coach called the team doctor to the field.

13. The doctor, a woman, began to check (his, him).

14. She listened to (his, him) heart.

15. She moved (his, him) arms and legs.

16. Finally, he moved (his, him) arm by himself.

17. He sat up. He waved to all of (our, us) in the audience.

18. The doctor helped (his, him) get up.

19. He put (his, him) arm around (hers, her) shoulders for support.

20. They walked slowly off the field. The announcer later told (our, us) the player was okay.

C. Look at the sentences using possessive pronouns and at those using object forms. What difference do you see in the structures of the sentences? Write a sentence or two expressing this difference. (*Hint:* Look at what comes after each pronoun.)

_____

_____

_____

_____

A GUIDE TO THE USE OF "IT'S" AND "ITS"

It's is a **contraction** that means "it is." It's always means "it is," and never means anything else, except occasionally "it has." **It's** belongs to the same family of contractions as "don't" and "doesn't" and "couldn't" and "won't."

Its, on the other hand, is a possessive pronoun. It always shows possession of a noun which usually follows it. Other members of this family include her, his, my, our, your. You will notice that these words, although they are called "possessive," do not have an apostrophe in them. Neither does **its** have an apostrophe to show possession. The confusion comes from the fact that we use an 's or an s' with nouns to show possession, but pronouns have their own special form to show possession. **Its** is a possessive pronoun and does not use an apostrophe.

EXERCISE 56

A. Practice using it's and its in the following sentences. Write the correct word, either possessive pronoun or contraction.

B. When you've filled in the blanks, notice that the paragraph does not seem to follow a very logical order. Rearrange the sentences and rewrite the paragraph so that the information is presented in better order.

Football is the name of the game in the United States. [1]_____ a very rough cross between rugby and soccer. In fact, almost all other countries in the world also play "football." North Americans call it by [2]_____ other name, soccer. [3]_____ just beginning to gain importance in the United States. Many school children, both male and female, now play soccer, thus increasing [4]_____ popularity in this country. [5]_____ not a sport for those who don't like to run. However, [6]_____ rules are very different from "American football." In other countries, [7]_____ name is "American football." In soccer, [8]_____ rules prohibit a player from touching the ball with his hands. In American football, [9]_____ necessary to touch the ball with the hands. In fact, [10]_____ impossible to play "football" without using the hands!

_____

_____

_____

_____

_____

_____

_____

We are the Contractions Family

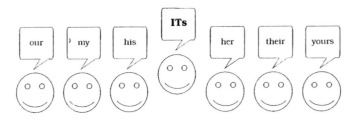

We are the Possessives Family

EXERCISE 57

A. Underline the correct object or possessive pronoun.

B. Above the word you underlined, write *P* if it is the possessive pronoun, *O* if it is the object pronoun.

[1](My, Me) family loves sports. [2](My, Me) father likes football the best. [3](His, Him) idea of relaxation is watching two teams move the ball down the field. I like to watch games with [4](his, him). He explains to [5](my, me) any rules I do not know. I try to remember [6](their, them). [7](My, me) brothers and I sometimes play football in the yard with [8](our, us) friends. [9](My, me) oldest brother will yell at [10](my, me) if I make a mistake.

"What's wrong with [11](your, you)?" Bob asks. "Girls can't play well," he says.

I reply, "Nobody taught [12](my, me) that rule."

He then says, "Let [13](my, me) explain it to [14](your, you)."

I am a quick learner. The game continues. Bob smiles at [15](my, me) when I follow the rules. [16](My, Me) ability improves with each game.

[17](My, Me) uncle prefers basketball. He played on [18](his, him) high school team in the 1950s. He was the star player one year. The local newspaper wrote many articles about [19](his, him). [20](His, Him) mother saved the articles. She put [21](their, them) in a scrapbook. One article has a picture of [22](his, him) shooting a basket. Today, Uncle Dick prefers to watch both men's and women's basketball teams shoot baskets on television. All players use [23](their, them) skills to make points. Some use [24](their, them) more than others. For example, Michael Jordan uses [25](his, him) ability to jump. [26](His, Him) teammates count on him to make a lot of points in a game. Chamique Holdsclaw is the Most Valuable Player of the college women's basketball tournament. Chamique uses [27](hers, her) strong legs to run up and down the court. All players must work hard to achieve [28](their, them) goals. [29](My, me) uncle always cheers for [30](their, them) when they score points. That makes the game more enjoyable for [31](his, him).

EXERCISE 58

Write the missing object or possessive pronoun in the blank.

1. Both individuals in a marriage must work at _____ relationship.

2. A wife must listen to _____ husband.

3. A husband must listen to _____ wife.

4. Sometimes, the husband may not understand _____ wife.

5. For example, he hears _____ say, "My job is so hard."

6. He tells _____, "Get a different job."

7. She then gets mad at _____. She says, "You never understand me!"

8. He doesn't understand that _____ wife wanted him to listen.

9. She wanted to talk about _____ problem at work.

10. _____ husband wanted to solve the problem, not listen.

11. The wife doesn't always understand _____ husband either.

12. He asks _____, "How was your day?"

13. She begins to tell _____ all the details.

14. Then he says, "I didn't ask _____ for a long story."

15. He just wanted _____ to say, "I had a good day."

16. This common problem bothers many couples. What can help _____?

17. Researchers in the United States are studying this communication problem. Researchers are also writing books about _____.

18. Hopefully, the books will help _____ overcome communication problems.

EXERCISE 59

Write the missing object or possessive pronoun in the blank.

Research shows that most American men do not listen to details. Do details bore (1)_____ ? Are (2)_____ minds moving too fast for details? Do men usually prefer to hear basic facts? Can we assume they also give basic facts? (3)_____ partner, Thuan, and I observed some men around (4)_____. This was an interesting subject for (5)_____ to study.

First, we observed Edward, whose construction company was building a home near (6)_____ college. Edward is (7)_____ friend's father. He was talking to (8)_____ crew of workers early one morning. Men and women worked on (9)_____ crew.

He asked one of (10)_____ workers, "Where is the cement we ordered?"

The worker began to explain, "Boss. I called (11)_____ yesterday. (12)_____ supplier has not delivered any cement this week. They said . . ."

Before the worker could continue, Edward interrupted. He said, "Just tell (13)_____ when the cement will arrive."

The worker responded, "They hope to deliver (14)_____ to (15)_____ this afternoon."

"Thank you," Edward replied. "Call (16)_____ when it arrives."

Thuan and I listened to (17)_____ conversation. It sounded like Edward wanted the facts only. Was he too busy to listen to (18)_____ worker? Was (19)_____ mind on something else? We didn't have enough information to decide.

95

EXERCISE 60

Write the missing object or possessive pronoun in the blank.

Thuan and I also observed some of (1)_____ male friends at the university. We listened to conversations the guys had with (2)_____ girlfriends. We noticed several things. First, when the girls talked for more than three minutes, some of (3)_____ boyfriends looked in another direction. Johnny provided a good example. We were sitting outside the classroom with Johnny and (4)_____ girlfriend, Sue. Thuan and I listened to (5)_____ conversation.

Sue began telling (6)_____ about her science class. Johnny looked at (7)_____ for about one minute. After that, (8)_____ eyes looked everywhere else, not at Sue. Finally, Sue said, "Johnny, are you listening to (9)_____?"

"What?" asked Johnny.

"I said, are you listening to (10)_____? I just told (11)_____ a funny story about science class."

Johnny replied, "Sorry. I guess I wasn't listening to (12)_____."

Thuan and I observed Johnny in other conversations. (13)_____ eye contact was usually weak. We also saw other guys do the same thing. We didn't understand (14)_____ behavior. Was it the details that bored (15)_____?

We noticed another thing about conversations between guys and girls. If the girl discussed a problem, (16)_____ boyfriend usually gave a quick solution. The boyfriend did not want to discuss the problem; he wanted to solve (17)_____. We saw this happen with Martha and Dan. Martha told Dan about a problem with (18)_____ English teacher, Mrs. Smith. Dan said quickly, "Go talk to the department chairman about (19)_____." Martha was not happy with (20)_____ comment.

EXERCISE 61

Write the missing pronoun in the blank.

1. I was born in Puerto Rico six years after _____ parents moved there.

2. _____ birth story is interesting.

3. _____ mother continued teaching at a small private school during her pregnancy.

4. Mom and Dad expected _____ baby on July 27.

5. During the summer, Mom and the other teachers painted and cleaned _____ school.

6. _____ dad was offered a special job that summer.

7. Dad's boss wanted _____ to teach in Belize, Central America.

8. _____ would return at the beginning of July.

9. Teaching this special marine science course was important to _____ father.

10. _____ decided to accept the special job.

11. Dad told Mom, "_____ will be home before the baby arrives."

12. _____ taught the class on an island many miles away from land.

13. There were no telephones. A boat brought the people _____ mail.

14. On July 3rd, _____ mother arrived home after working at the school.

15. The cat ran into the house with something in _____ mouth.

16. Mom called the cat: "Nora! Come here girl. What is in _____ mouth?"

17. Then _____ reached for the cat.

18. At that moment, Mom felt something happen inside _____ body.

19. "Oh no! _____ is the baby, three weeks early!" Mom cried.

20. Dad's baby daughter arrived before _____ could get home.

EXERCISE 62

Write the missing pronoun in the blank.

The month after I was born, (1)_____ parents bought a new house. (2)_____ was located outside of the town of San German, Puerto Rico. (3)_____ was about ten years old. Mom and Dad liked the house because (4)_____ was made of natural wood. Many of the houses in San German were made of concrete blocks. (5)_____ parents were happy with the change. From the house, (6)_____ could see mountains and fields. (7)_____ loved the beautiful view and the clean air. Dad worked in the yard during (8)_____ free time. Sometimes, he drove into the mountains to find tropical plants for (9)____ garden. Dad was proud of (10)_____ garden and yard.

EXERCISE 63

Write the missing pronoun in the blank.

A town needs retail stores to make (1)_____ a successful town. A town needs to provide (2)_____ citizens with products for (3)_____ homes, gardens, automobiles, and personal needs. Sometimes these stores are located downtown. Business people can easily shop for the items (4)_____ need during lunch breaks or after work. If the stores are smaller, (5)_____ usually offer (6)_____ customers personalized service. In many towns, citizens shop in large department stores for all (7)_____ needs. Sometimes large stores are located in shopping centers or malls beside smaller specialized stores. This arrangement makes (8)_____ easy for shoppers to find everything under one roof. However, (9)_____ don't get much personalized service in the large stores.

CHAPTER 12
Reflexive Pronouns

Reflexive pronouns refer to their antecedents for clarification and/or emphasis. Many of their uses are also idiomatic. Here are examples of each:

I have been dressing myself since I was four years old. (Idiomatic usage: to dress oneself)

She told herself she would not cry at the movie. (emphasis)

We understood ourselves to be in great danger. (clarification)

Most idiomatic expressions with reflexive verbs begin with the words "by" or "to." For example:

I want to do it by myself! ("By myself" is a very common expression.)

He married so that he didn't have to live by himself anymore.

She mumbled to herself as she left the room.

To use a reflexive pronoun in place of an appropriate is an error in usage.

Incorrect: Please email either John or myself with your vote.

Correct: Please email either John or me with your vote.

Incorrect: He hurt hisself. (There is no such word as "hisself.")

Correct: He hurt himself.

EXERCISE 64

Underline the correct reflexive pronoun.

Example: Some stories help us understand (<u>ourselves</u>, themselves).

1. The characters in some stories learn about (themselves, themself).

2. The husband in "Cathedral" was unsure of (himself, herself).

3. He stayed home by (himself, herself).

4. His wife did things by (himself, herself). Sometimes she included her husband.

5. She wanted her blind friend to visit. The blind man lived by (himself, themselves).

6. Robert, the blind man, traveled on the train by (themselves, himself).

7. The husband didn't want to involve (himself, herself) with a blind man.

8. The husband said, "Go by (herself, yourself) to pick him up at the train station."

9. She happily went by (himself, herself).

10. Robert and the wife laughed to (themselves, themself) as they arrived at the house.

11. The jealous, unhappy husband sat inside by (himself, herself).

12. He watched them. He thought to (herself, himself), "How can a blind man travel alone?"

13. The wife told Robert, "Make (yourselves, yourself) at home."

14. Later, Robert and the husband watched television by (themself, themselves).

15. Robert had trouble understanding the program about cathedrals by (themselves, himself).

16. The husband explained what cathedrals were. He began to involve (himself, themselves) in the blind man's world.

17. They drew a picture of a cathedral together with their eyes closed. The husband wasn't by (herself, himself) anymore.

EXERCISE 65

Underline the correct reflexive pronoun.

Parents teach their kids the rules. However, kids get [1](himself, themselves) into trouble by breaking the rules. Five-year-old Ioanna is a good example. She usually plays by [2](herself, herselves) in the house. She knows she cannot go outside by [3](himself, herself). Ioanna's mother works by [4](herself, himself) in the office by the kitchen. Usually, they keep [5](themself, themselves) busy for an hour or so. Then they do something together. One day, Ioanna got [6](herself, themselves) into a lot of trouble. She broke the rules. She decided to dress [7](himself, herself) up in her mother's clothes. Then she put lipstick all over [8](themselves, herself) and the walls of the bedroom. Her mother found her and laughed to [9](herself, themselves). To Ioanna she said, "Do not play by [10](yourselves, yourself) in my bedroom. You know the rules." Ioanna cleaned up the mess by [11](herself, themselves).

EXERCISE 66

Underline the correct reflexive pronoun.

Following all their parents' rules is difficult for children. Children often think they can take care of [1](themselves, theirselves). Mohammed is like that. His parents don't want him to ride his bike to the park by [2](himself, herself). He's only ten years old, so it is dangerous. One day he took off by [3](themselves, himself); he didn't tell anyone. He met a friend at the park. They stayed at the park by [4](themselves, themself) until late in the afternoon. Mohammed's mother began to worry. She drove [5](himself, herself) around the neighborhood looking for him. She almost drove [6](himself, herself) crazy because she couldn't find him. Finally, she saw him riding home by [7](themselves, himself). She pulled up next to him and said, "What are you doing out here by [8](yourselves, yourself)?!!" She was glad he was safe. He learned to follow the rules!

EXERCISE 67

Write the correct reflexive pronoun in the blank and in the blanks in front of the sentence numbers. Write E if the reflexive is used for emphasis, C if it is used for clarity, and I if it is used idiomatically.

Example: This book is about a boy. He finds <u>himself</u> going on an adventure.

_____ 1. Jim lives in the 1800s and works in his parents' hotel. He likes to work by

_____ .

_____ 2. An old sailor comes to the hotel, singing to _____ .

_____ 3. The old sailor spends time by _____ .

_____ 4. The old sailor drinks _____ to sleep every day.

_____ 5. He dies, and Jim finds _____ looking in the man's old sea chest.

_____ 6. Jim's mother takes some of the man's money for _____ , to pay his

bills.

_____ 7. Jim finds a treasure map. Jim and some men decide to get the treasure

for _____ .

_____ 8. They need a ship to get _____ to the island.

_____ 9. Jim goes by _____ to find a man named Long John Silver.

_____ 10. Silver asks, "Did you come here by _____ ?"

_____ 11. Jim answers, "Yes, I came by _____ . Here is a letter."

_____ 12. "Let's go see the ship for _____ ," says Silver.

_____ 13. They sail from England. The men keep _____ busy on the ship.

_____ 14. Jim keeps _____ busy as the cabin boy for the ship.

_____ 15. The cook works by _____ preparing the meals.

_____ 16. The sailors fill _____ with apples and potatoes.

EXERCISE 68

Write the correct reflexive pronoun in the blank.

Jim discovers by (1)_____ that the sailors are pirates. One night he goes on deck to get an apple for (2)_____, but there are no apples. When he hears some voices, he hides (3)_____ from the men. Nearby, Long John Silver and some of the sailors are talking among (4)_____, discussing how they will take control of the ship. Silver says to his men, "You know (5)_____ I'm a gentleman of fortune." This means Silver is a pirate. Jim says to (6)_____, "If Silver finds me, how will I get (7)_____ out of danger?" The men are drinking. One man says, "Let's drink to (8)_____ and our good fortune." Just then the moonlight falls on Jim's hiding place. Then the sailor on watch cries out, "Land! Land ho!" No one sees Jim standing by (9)_____ in the corner.

EXERCISE 69

A. Write the correct pronoun (subject, object, possessive, or reflexive) in the blank.

B. Above the pronoun in the blank, write S, O, P, or R to indicate which type pronoun you used.

The captain calls all the men and discusses where (1)_____ should leave the ship. Everyone is happy. (2)_____ have arrived at the island on the map and will search for the treasure. To celebrate (3)_____ arrival, the captain orders drinks for everyone. The captain and two other men decide to have drinks by (4)_____. The three men ask Jim to join (5)_____. Jim explains that Silver and some of the other men are dangerous pirates. (6)_____ want Jim to get more information. The captain tells Jim to take care of (7)_____ around the pirates. Jim tells the men, "I can take care of (8)_____."

EXERCISE 70

A. Write the correct pronoun (subject, object, possessive, or reflexive) in the blank.

B. Above the pronoun in the blank, write the pronoun's referent.

My friends, Mary and Paul, traveled to Hawaii for the first time last summer. (1)_____ visited the island of Maui. (2)_____ is a beautiful island, and Mary took many photographs of the scenery. (3)_____ is a photographer. Paul went scuba diving, and (4)_____ saw a shark! Mary asked (5)_____ if (6)_____ was scared when he saw the shark. Paul said he wasn't scared at all! Paul and Mary saw many interesting things on (7)_____ trip. (8)_____ drove to the town of Hana, and (9)_____ also drove to the top of a volcano that was 10,000 feet high. When Paul and Mary left Maui, they promised (10)_____ that they would return some day.

CHAPTER 13
Relative Pronouns
Who, Whom, Which, That

We use the pronouns who, whom, and which to form questions, but as relative pronouns, they are also used to build sentences. When we use them in this way, we are really putting two sentences together as one. Look at this example:

John likes to play baseball. John is my friend.

If we combine these with who, we get a new sentence: John, who is my friend, likes to play baseball. (Notice that we do not repeat "John" since "John" is replaced by "who.")

Correct: John, who is my friend, likes to play baseball.

Incorrect: John who is my friend likes to play baseball.

■ Use who to refer to people or animals with names. Here are some examples:

The man who lives next door cuts the grass early in the morning.

Lady, who barks when the lawn mower is running, is a friendly dog.

■ Use which to refer to animals, things, and sometimes groups of people. It is best to use which in nonrestrictive clauses. Nonrestrictive clauses follow a specific name for an animal, thing, or group of people. Nonrestrictive clauses modify a noun or noun phrase without being necessary. Nonrestrictive clauses could be deleted from a sentence without greatly changing the meaning. A nonrestrictive clause is usually set off with commas.

Examples: The Statue of Liberty, which is located on Ellis Island, welcomes all to the U.S.

The book on Kennedy, which I bought, is so heavy.

We hope the baseball team, which plays tonight, wins the game.

Politicians, who are in charge of running the government, work in the capitol.

Here "who are in charge of running the government" is marked as a nonrestrictive element by the commas around it. The meaning of "politicians" is general. The sentence means that *all* politicians work in the capitol. If we remove the nonrestrictive element *who are in charge of running the government*, the sentence still means politicians work in the capitol. Commas are needed.

■ Use that to refer to animals, things, and sometimes to groups of people. Today we often use that in place of the word "whom," which is the object form of "who." As the English language changes over time, some words are used seldom and others are dropped entirely. This is what is happening to the word "whom." Hardly anyone knows how to use it correctly, and it often sounds rather pretentious when it is used correctly. Consider this sentence:

He is the man whom my father warned me about.

This sentence is the combination of these two: "He is the man. My father warned me about the man." Note that the "man" is in the object position in the second sentence, so the object form of "who" would be used. That form is "whom." We usually hear it this way:

He is the man that my father warned me about.

Whether you try to learn the correct usage of "whom" by studying a grammar hand-book or whether you decide to do what's easier and use "that" will depend on you, your instructor, and your needs.

EXERCISE 71

Underline the correct pronoun (who, which, that).

Example: People enjoy eating in restaurants (who, <u>that</u>) offer a variety of dishes.

1. Florida residents (who, that) live in populated areas can find good restaurants.

2. Some people choose restaurants (that, which) are located nearby.

3. For those (who, whom) like seafood, there is a wide variety.

4. Fred likes to go to restaurants (that, who) are located near his home.

5. He has found many local restaurants (who, that) serve delicious dinners.

6. Some people will drive to a restaurant (that, which) is located far away.

7. My best friend, (who, which) lives in Tampa, drives eighty miles to a restaurant in Orlando.

8. She likes the Hard Rock Café, (who, which) is located near a popular tourist attraction.

9. There are people in Florida (which, who) eat out every day!

10. In Florida, Fred is the man (who, whom) the restaurant owners love.

EXERCISE 72

A. Underline the correct pronoun (who, which, that).

B. Below each sentence, write the two sentences that this sentence was built from. The first one is done as an example.

1. John loves to go to restaurants (which, that) serve spicy food.

   John loves to go to restaurants. The restaurants serve spicy food.

2. He likes tacos with chilis (that, who) set his mouth on fire.

   _____

3. Indian curry, (which, that) is hot and spicy, makes him smile.

   _____

4. If John gets a pizza, he adds red pepper, (which, who) the waiter brings to the table.

   _____

5. He must have a stomach (who, that) is very strong.

   _____

6. John is a person (who, which) never gets sick from food.

   _____

7. He can eat everything (that, which) the waiter brings.

   _____

8. John also brings spicy food to work.

   _____

9. He brought some peppers (that, who) burned our tongues.

   _____

10. We love the smell (that, which) comes out of the microwave into the hall.

    _____

EXERCISE 73

Combine the two sentences to make one using a who, that, or which clause. The first one is done as an example.

1. The food called "Tex-Mex" is spicy. I like the spicy food.

   Example: I like the spicy food called "Tex-Mex."

2. Students need money for tuition. They can apply for work-study scholarships.

   _____

3. She asked to see the dress. The dress was in the store's window.

   _____

4. Thomas Jefferson was an American statesman. Thomas Jefferson had many other interests.

   _____

5. She is the friend. The friend always gets me into trouble.

   _____

6. My idea was simple. I shared my idea.

   _____

7. The Civil War was an unpopular war. The war was really motivated by greed.

   _____

8. The movie is well known over the world. The movie is _Star Wars_.

   _____

9. The basket was full of newspapers. The newspapers were old.

   _____

10. They are the people. I told you about the people.

   _____

1. Choose a piece of your own writing, a paragraph in length or longer, that you can edit for correct pronoun usage.

2. Underline each pronoun you have used. Look for subject and object pronouns, possessive pronouns, reflexive pronouns, and relative pronouns.

3. Examine each pronoun to be certain that you have used the correct form. Look at its position in the sentence, and also pay close attention to the distinction between its and it's.

4. Make sure that each pronoun has a clear referent. Can you easily identify the word to which the pronoun refers? Does the pronoun agree with its referent?

PART VI

PREPOSITIONS

A **preposition** is a word that helps show a relationship between two ideas in a sentence. Prepositions are followed by a noun or pronoun. Together they make up a prepositional phrase. Prepositional phrases may also contain adjectives.

- Some prepositions indicate location and time. Note the meaning of the prepositional phrases in this sentence:

He worked on his father's farm in the country after school was out.

on his father's farm (describes the place where he worked)

in the country (describes the location of the farm)

after school (describes when he worked)

- Some prepositions also function as other parts of speech. Notice the use of the word *to:*

John went **to the office** at eight o'clock. He had **to work** on a project.

In the first sentence, to *the office* is a prepositional phrase indicating a location. In the second sentence, to *work* is an infinitive verb phrase.

- Here is a list of the most common prepositions: at, for, from, in, of, to, with. To help you remember prepositions of location, think of anything a jet can do to a cloud: A jet can go in, above, beyond, beside, around, behind, through, inside a cloud.

- Choose and use the prepositions in, on, and at carefully when referring to time and place:

Time:

in a period of time—in a few days, in an hour

in a particular month or year—in June, in 1998

in a period of time during the day—in the morning

on a specific day—on Monday, on Sept. 24, on Veterans' Day

on time

at a definite time—at 9:00, at lunch time

Place:

> inside a specific place—in the desk drawer, in his pocket, in the room
>
> at a specific place—at the park, at my mother's home
>
> on top of something—on the desk, on the mountain, on your street

- Sometimes, two speakers of English will use different prepositions to mean the same thing. Different areas in the United States use different prepositional phrases. For example, some people will say, "Get in line." Others will say, "Get on line." Both mean the same thing—form a line. And today, people often mean "get on the Internet" when they say, "get online."

Exercise 74

Read the following paragraph. Underline all prepositional phrases and circle the prepositions. Remember that some sentences may contain more than one prepositional phrase. You will find ten prepositional phrases in all.

I began studying English in 1995. The English class I took was offered by the public school in the evening. Many of the students in my class were from other countries. I went to class with my husband because he was also learning English. Our English skills improved very quickly. Now my husband teaches a basic English class for his co-workers at his office. I am proud that his English has improved so much!

EXERCISE 75

Underline the correct preposition.

Example: Studying (<u>in</u>, on) the summer is a challenge.

1. (At, In) my university, some summer classes meet every day for six weeks.

2. Those classes meet (in, at) the morning or afternoon for one hour and twenty minutes.

3. (In, At) the evening, classes meet for two hours and thirty minutes.

4. The professors give assignments every day. We turn them (in, on) the next day.

5. This means we study every day (in, on) our free time.

6. Some students take two or three classes (in, on) the summer.

7. They have to study all the time. My friend Mark studies (at, in) two in the morning.

8. He is taking 12 credits. Assignments are (in, on) his mind all the time.

9. He can't sleep late (in, on) the morning.

10. He comes (in, on) early from dates with his girlfriend.

11. He can only be (at, in) work 20 hours a week.

12. He doesn't mind this sacrifice. He is (in, on) his early twenties.

13. He will have time to have fun later. Now he wants to concentrate (in, on) his studies.

14. The short semester will be over (on, in) June.

15. I wish that were (at, in) a few days, not weeks!

16. We have so much work to do (at, in) a short time.

17. We have to turn (on, in) a 600-word essay tomorrow.

18. I will complete my essay (in, at) 10:00 tonight.

19. Then I will work (on, in) my math assignment.

20. I don't know if I'll study (in, on) the summer next year.

EXERCISE 76

Write ten sentences with prepositional phrases that describe your life at work, at school, or at home. Use the common prepositions from the lists at the beginning of this chapter.

_____

_____

_____

_____

_____

_____

_____

_____

_____

_____

EDITING IN CONTEXT—PREPOSITIONS

1. Choose a piece of writing, a paragraph or longer, that you can edit for correct preposition usage.

2. Read carefully and underline each preposition in the piece of writing that you have chosen.

3. Examine each preposition. Should you use a preposition of location, time, or place? Did you choose the correct preposition? If you are unsure about your choice, check in a dictionary that lists expressions used with prepositions.

PART VII

SENTENCE STRUCTURES

■ ■ ■

CHAPTER 14

Units of Construction

The word is the basic building block of any language. After the word comes the phrase, then the clause, and finally the sentence.

Word + Word = Phrase

Subject + Verb = Clause

Independent Clause = Sentence

The number of words does not necessarily determine whether or not a group of words is a sentence. For instance, a sentence may be two words:

He is.

It isn't.

They weren't.

I didn't.

These sentences, however short, satisfy the two conditions necessary for a group of words to be a sentence:

1. They make some sort of sense as a single unit.

2. They have a complete subject and a complete verb.

On the other hand, for all its words, this word group is not a sentence:

Golf, fishing, hiking, water skiing, roller blading, bicycling.

Neither is this word group:

Because of all the nice things you do, the sweet ways you have, and the kindness of your heart. (Again, length is not strength.)

But when we look at the example above, we DO see a noun or two and we see several verbs, so why isn't it a sentence? The answer is that it begins with a **subordinate conjunction**, the word **because**. When one of these words begins a word group, that word group must be followed by a comma and an independent clause.

I love you. (Independent Clause)

Because of all the nice things you do, the sweet ways you have, and the kindness of your heart (all this is "dependent" because of the subordinate conjunction at the beginning), I love you. (The addition of the independent clause "I love you" makes this now a complete sentence.)

Common Subordinate Conjunctinos

because	although	if	since	when
while	after	until	before	despite
in spite of	even though	as		

Additionally in English, we have four types of sentences based on their function: declarative, imperative, interrogative, and exclamatory.

Declarative: Learning to speak and write in a second language is difficult.

Imperative: Stay in college and earn your degree.

Interrogative: Will the stores be open on Christmas Eve?

Exclamatory: What an expensive diamond ring she was wearing!

Chapter 15

Types of Sentences Based on Coordination and Subordination

Sentences may be of the following types: simple, complex, compound, compound-complex.

- **Simple Sentences:** A simple sentence has a simple subject and verb. "I love you" is a simple sentence. "I love you and respect you" is also a simple sentence although this simple sentence now has two verbs.

- **Complex Sentences:** The independent clause "I love you" is a complete sentence on its own. If a person said, "I love you," that is a recognizable complete thought. If we combine the simple sentence "I love you" with the dependent clause "Because of all . . ." we get a sort of sentence and a half.

Complete Sentence + Subordinate Conjunction + Sentence = 1½ sentence = Complex Sentence

A complex sentence is composed of an independent clause and a dependent clause. Here are some other examples:

When it rains, I carry my umbrella.
(When it rains = subordinate conjunction + sentence) + (I carry my umbrella = complete sentence.)

The music played while the crowd danced.
(The music played = complete sentence) + (while the crowd danced = subordinate conjunction + sentence.)

Notice the punctuation difference between these two complex sentences. In the first complex sentence, the dependent clause is written first and followed by a comma. But when the independent clause is written first, there is no comma.

This is also a good way to know whether or not you've written a fragment, which is usually considered a major sentence structure error. If your sentence begins with a subordinate conjunction (as mine does in this sentence), there must be a comma or else you have very likely written a fragment.

- **Compound Sentences:** The independent clause "I love you" can also be combined with another independent clause like "You love me." When we combine these two, instead of a sentence and a half, we get two sentences in one: a compound sentence.

Complete Sentence + Complete Sentence = 2 Sentences = Compound Sentence

Consider the two independent clauses: I love you + You love me. Compound sentences **must** have glue to put them together, however. That glue cannot be simply a comma. We need punctuation (a comma) as well as words called coordinating conjunctions, or, called by their acronym, fanboys. Fanboys is a mnemonic device to help you remember what each of the letters in this word stands for.

F   A   N   B   O   Y   S

For   And   Nor   But   Or   Yet   So

When we join two complete sentences with one of these words, we use a comma before the conjunction.

I love you, **for** you love me.

I love you, **and** you love me.

I don't love you, **nor** do you love me.

I love you, **but** you don't love me.

Do I love you, **or** do you love me?

I don't love you, **yet** you love me.

I love you, **so** you love me.

Another way to compound (put together) sentences is to use a semicolon between the two independent clauses.

I love you; you love me.

We often use a colon (:) to combine two independent clauses when the second clause seems to be a result of the first:

I love you: You love me. (Notice the capital letter.)

A combination of a compound sentence and a complex sentence is called a compound-complex sentence.

Compound Sentence + Complex Sentence = Compound-Complex Sentence

If I loved you, you would love me, and we would be happy. (Dependent + Independent + Independent)

CHAPTER 16
Questions

Simple yes/no questions are formed in English by adding an appropriate helping verb, changing the main verb to the infinitive form, and altering the order of the words in a declarative sentence. Here are examples:

Sentence: I have a friend.

Question: Do I have a friend? (Because "have" is in the present tense and because "I" is singular, the helping verb "do" is used to form that question.)

Sentence: John is the instructor.

Question: Is John the instructor? ("To be" verbs in present tense do not use helping verbs.)

Sentence: Mary goes to Europe each year.

Question: Does Mary go to Europe each year?

Sentence: Selena visited Mexico last week.

Question: Did Selena visit Mexico last week?

The "wh" questions ask for information rather than a simple "yes" or "no" answer. Who, whom, how, what, when, where, which, whose, why are common "wh" question words. Study these examples:

How do you know the way to his house so well? (Notice the addition of "how" to the regular question form.)

What is your name? (As in regular "yes/no" questions, the helping verb is not used with BE verbs.)

Where do you live?

Which house is yours?

Why are you here?

When did you arrive?

How long have you known him?

Whose car is parked out front?

Whom did you say called?

Notice how we form the "wh" question based on the position in the sentence where the information we want to ask about is located.

This year the farmers planted alfalfa in their fields to get the greatest yield from their crops.

1	2	3	4	5	6	7

1. (when) When did the farmers plant alfalfa? (this year)

2. (who) Who planted alfalfa this year? (the farmers)

3. (what) What did the farmers do this year? (planted alfalfa)

4. (what) What did the farmers plant? (alfalfa)

5. (where) Where did the farmers plant alfalfa? (in their fields)

6. (why) Why did the farmers plant alfalfa? (to get the greatest yield)

7. (whose) Whose crops are they? ("their" crops = the farmers' crops)

Other questions we could ask are: Which crop did they plant? Whose fields are they?

EXERCISE 77

Form yes/no questions from the sentences written below.

Example: John went to Los Angeles (Did John go to Los Angeles?)

1. John had a business trip.

   _____

2. He traveled on Tuesday.

   _____

3. The weather was bad that day.

   _____

4. John's flight was delayed one hour.

   _____

5. The plane could not fly in the storm.

   _____

6. John spent time reading a comic book.

   _____

7. He fell asleep while he was reading.

   _____

8. John didn't hear the announcement to board his flight.

   _____

9. John's flight left without him.

   _____

10. John had to go to the ticket counter to ask for a new ticket.

    _____

EXERCISE 78

Form "wh" questions from the sentences in Exercise 77 by using the following question words:

1. Who

   _____

2. When

   _____

3. What

   _____

4. Whose

   _____

5. Why

   _____

6. How

   _____

7. When

   _____

8. What

   _____

9. Whose

   _____

10. Where

   _____

EXERCISE 79

Pretend that you are a detective on a very mysterious criminal case. The only thing you know is what is given in the paragraph that follows. Formulate at least 8 "wh" questions.

A house was broken into sometime in the early morning hours today. Police are not sure how many suspects there might be, and they have not as yet discovered what was stolen, if anything. The homeowners did not appear to be home when the crime was committed.

_____

_____

_____

_____

_____

_____

_____

_____

_____

_____

CHAPTER 17
Negative Sentences

Forming negative declarative sentences is much like forming questions. Study these examples:

1. She wanted three children.

   Negative: She did not want three children.

2. They are renting an apartment.

   Negative: They are not renting an apartment.

3. The movie star has been hiding in Aspen, Colorado.

   Negative: The movie star has not been hiding in Aspen, Colorado.

In sentence 1, the action verb is in the past tense, so we must add a helping verb matching the past tense, change the past tense main verb "wanted" to the infinitive form "want," and alter the positions of the words in the sentence.

In sentence 2, the "be" verb does not take a helping verb in negative sentences just as it does not in questions.

In sentence 3, the helping verb is already present as it is used in the present perfect continuous tense. In that case, the negative word only is needed.

EXERCISE 80

Change each sentence to the negative.

Example: Researchers have used Carl Jung's theories to create personality profiles.

Researchers haven't used Carl Jung's theories to create personality profiles.

1. Jung believed there were four ways to look at personality.

   _____

2. He described the first way.

   _____

3. He looked at how people get energy from the world.

   _____

4. Some people are extroverted.

   _____

5. They talk and move a lot.

   _____

6. They get energy by being with other people.

   _____

7. They ask a lot of questions.

   _____

8. Extroverted students jump into assignments.

   _____

9. Other people are introverted.

   _____

10. They talk less and are less active.

    _____

11. They get energy from quiet and solitude.

_____

12. They are excellent listeners.

_____

13. Introverts like to remain quiet in the classroom.

_____

14. Introverts avoid group work.

_____

15. Introverts and extroverts are quite different.

_____

EXERCISE 81

A. Change each verb to the negative in the space above the verb.

                   didn't study

Example: Jung ~~studied~~ a second way to understand personality.

      The second way Jung classified personality is how people perceive the world. Some people have a strong sensory perception. They pay attention to details; they can "see the trees." These individuals prefer to study concrete ideas before abstract ones. They need logic and order in their lives. In a math class, they want step-by-step instructions. Interestingly, memorizing facts is easy for them. Actors and actresses may have strong sensory perception. Other people are more intuitive. They find details boring; they can "see the forest." Frequently, they come up with an answer in a different way. They like using their imagination and being creative. The big picture comes in clearly for these individuals. Studies show that 80 percent of college professors are intuitive. Most community college students are sensory oriented. This difference can cause miscommunication in the classroom. Professors need to understand their students' personalities and learning styles.

B. This paragraph sounds choppy because the writer used mostly simple sentences. Rewrite the paragraph, making compound, complex, and compound-complex sentences wherever you can. Pay close attention to punctuation.

_____

_____

_____

_____

_____

_____

EXERCISE 82

A. Write the correct preposition (in, on, at, to, of, from, with).

B. Change each sentence to the negative statement wherever it is possible.

The third personality type comes (1)_____ the way people make decisions. Individuals who rely (2)_____ their brains to make decisions are thinkers. These thinkers deal (3)_____ life logically. They look (4)_____ life as cause-effect relationships. Most men fall (5)_____ this category. Perhaps that is why they like to solve problems. The other group relies (6)_____ the heart to make decisions. These people, called feelers, see the human side (7)_____ a topic. They will go (8)_____ the end (9)_____ the earth to make their values known. Most women are (10)_____ this category. Judgments come (11)_____ the feelers' values and beliefs. Feelers tell everything (12)_____ the ones they love. They also tell their professors everything that is happening (13)_____ their lives.

The last way to define personality is by looking (14)_____ the person's attitude toward life. Those who judge everything prefer life (15)_____ no surprises. If something isn't (16)_____ the plan, they don't want it. Students (17)_____ this group tell their professors, "That test question wasn't (18)_____ the review sheet." They also always want to know their grade point average. Others are guided by a strong perception (19)_____ their environment. They like to be involved (20)_____ surprises. They do not write anything (21)_____ their calendars. They do not wear watches (22)_____ their wrists. They perceive time (23)_____ their bodies. These students may not come (24)_____ class for a test. They say (25)_____ the professor, "I was sleeping. Can I come (26)_____ your office to take the test?"

EXERCISE 83

A. Underline the complete verb in each negative sentence or question. Label above the words in the verb phrase "helping verb" or "main verb."

B. This exercise contains a variety of types of sentences. In front of the sentence number, write D for declarative (statement), I for interrogative (question), E for exclamatory (excited), and M for Imperative (command).

_____ 1. A presidential race in the United States is not always a pretty sight.

_____ 2. How many political parties do we have in the United States?

_____ 3. I'll bet you didn't know that we actually have more than two.

_____ 4. Did you know that besides the Republicans and Democrats we also have other parties?

_____ 5. These minor parties usually don't have much effect on the outcome of the elections.

_____ 6. I have never voted for any party other than Republican or Democrat.

_____ 7. How many political parties do you have in Mexico, Beatriz?

_____ 8. Are the elections in Mexico well organized or not?

_____ 9. I can't believe how insulting the candidates can sometimes be to each other!

_____ 10. I don't believe candidates should sling mud on each other.

_____ 11. Don't they have to get along after the elections are over?

_____ 12. Have you ever thought about the ill effects of this negative campaigning?

_____ 13. Have you known other countries' candidates to be so cruel to each other?

_____ 14. The United States' presidential races have not historically been calm events.

C. 1. Combine sentence number 1 with sentence 14 in a compound sentence structure.

_____

_____

2. To make a complex sentence, attach the dependent clause _although we have other political parties_ onto either the beginning or ending of sentence 5, punctuating correctly.

_____

_____

3. Make sentence 6 a complex sentence by adding a dependent clause that *you create*.

_____

_____

D. Write a paragraph about the presidential elections in your country. Be sure you use at least one compound sentence, one complex sentence, and one compound-complex sentence.

_____

_____

_____

_____

_____

_____

_____

Editing in Context—Sentence Structures

1. Choose a piece of writing that you can edit for sentence structure. This should be a piece of writing that is at least a paragraph in length, if not longer.
2. Carefully read each sentence separately, asking the following questions:
   - Does the sentence make sense as a single unit?
   - Does the sentence have both a clear subject and a complete verb?
   - Have you used a subordinate conjunction at the beginning of the sentence to form a dependent clause? If so, have you placed a comma and a complete sentence after the dependent clause?
   - Are there any sentences that you could combine to make your writing style sound more sophisticated? Experienced writers often use a variety of sentence types to make their writing sound more interesting to their readers. Have you used many simple sentences? If so, you might want to consider combining some of your sentences so that you include a few different sentence types. You might try reading your writing out loud to see how it "sounds" when you read it. At first, it may be difficult to determine whether it "sounds" right, but the more you read writing (both to yourself and out loud), and the more you listen to the patterns of sentences in English, the better your own writing will become.

Internet Resources

The Internet offers many websites where you can get help as you learn more about the English language. Also consider using search engines, such as Dogpile, to find information because websites may disappear. Here is a list of some of those sites:

ESL Resources for Students

http://owl.english.purdue/esl/ESL-student.html

Dave Sperling's ESL Café

http://www.daveslcafe.com

Self-Study Quizzes for ESL

http://a4esl.org/q/h

English Grammar Links for ESL Students

http://www.gl.umbc.edu/~kpokoy1/grammar1.htm

ESL Magazine

http://www.eslmag.com

Randall's ESL Cyber-Listening Lab

http://www.esl-lab.com

Interesting Things for ESL Students

http://www.manythings.org

English for All

http://myefa.org/login.cfm

Guide to ESL-English Language Programs in the USA

http://www.esl.com

Dogpile Search Engine (enter a specific grammar term or "ESL" to find more websites)

http://www.dogpile.com

List Other Internet Sites You Find Helpful:

Answer Key

To help you check your answers, sometimes the word before or after the answer is also included.

Exercise 1:
1. student-count, class-count, mountains-count 2. mountain climbing-noncount, strength-noncount, courage-noncount 3. vacation-count, summer-count, peak-count 4. trip-count, climb-count, journal-count 5. Students-count, writing-noncount, English-noncount, year-count

Exercise 2 A:
1. programs 2. home 3. television 4. places 5. countries 6. customs 7. birthdays 8. meals 9. traditions 10. things 11. mountain 12. birds 13. lions 14. eyes 15. television

Exercise 2 B: Answers may vary

Exercise 3:
1. places 2. tour 3. buildings 4. tourists 5. elevator 6. visitors 7. island 8. boats 9. city 10. program 11. thousands 12. end 13. seconds 14. place 15. desert 16. plants 17. color 18. color 19. sky 20. animals 21. shape 22. rock 23. examples

Exercise 4 A:
1. attractions 2. shows 3. animals 4. bears 5. lions 6. owl 7. bottles 8. teenagers 9. men 10. snakes 11. women 12. female 13. feathers 14. bats 15. grandparents 16. program 17. cage 18. camera 19. time 20. animals 21. trip

Exercise 4 B:
1. no "a" before popular 2. these 3. variety of (prepositional phrases like this always take the plural noun) 4. two 5. Several 6. An 7. All animals means we need more than one "bottle" hence bottles 8. No "a" or other word to indicate ONE 9. nothing to indicate ONE 10. a 11. nothing to indicate only one 12. a 13. he has more than one feather-the verb is "are" 14. the verb "navigate" takes a plural subject 15. all the other nouns are plural 16. the verb is "makes"-takes a singular subject 17. A monkey is one 18. each always means one 19. This 20. see all the animals 21. a

Exercise 5 A:
1. homework-noncount 2. Mathematics-noncount 3. problems-count 4. science-noncount 5. children-count 6. day-count 7. laundry-noncount 8. clothes-count 9. shoes/socks-count 10. toys-count 11. things-count 12. Responsibility-noncount 13. possessions-count 14. property-noncount 15. habits-count

Exercise 5 B:
4. the sciences, 6. all the days of the week 12. Responsibilities are other things

Exercise 6 A:
1. individuals 2. parents 3. affection 4. nature 5. love 6. kisses 7. things 8. cards 9. family 10. feelings 11. day 12. partners 13. Trust 14. children 15. generation 16. process 17. time

Exercise 6 B:
1. more than one individual 2. the verb "love" takes a plural subject 3. noncount noun 4. one mother = one nature 5. noncount noun 6. other nouns in series are plural 7. count noun, more than one 8. no article and other noun is in plural 9. our = one family 10. verb "mature" takes plural noun 11. ONE 12. We = more than one partner 13. noncount 14. verb "arrive" takes plural subject 15. our children constitute only ONE generation 16. This 17. noncount

Exercise 6 C:

1. "other" is used with plural nouns or to signify "either": Other individuals OR this one or the other one 2. "them" implies that we give more than one card; also, presents is in the plural too 3. "A" 4. "This" is used with singular nouns,

Exercise 6 D: Answers may vary

Exercise 7:

1. the/the 2. the 3. a 4. an 5. the 6. a 7. a 8. the 9. An/the 10. a 11. an 12. the 13. the 14. an 15. the 16. a 17. the

Exercise 7 B 1: Answers may vary

Exercise 7 B 2:

a lot

Exercise 7 B 3: Answers may vary

Exercise 8 A:

1. the afternoon 2. an afternoon 3. a soap 4. the lives 5. the mistakes 6. the evil 7. the way 8. a man 9. a soap 10. an important 11. a soap 12. a young 13. The program

Exercise 8 B 1: Answers may vary

Exercise 8 B 2:

mistakes

Exercise 8 B 3: Answers may vary

Exercise 9: Answers may vary

Exercise 10 A & B:

1. a 2. X-pl 3. X-nc 4. X-pl 5. a 6. a 7. X-nc 8. a/a 9. the/X-pl 10. X-nc/the 11. the 12. a/a 13. the 14. X-nc 15. a 16. the 17. X-pl 18. the 19. a/a 20. X-nc 21. X-nc

Exercise 11:

   2. There are two types of articles, definite and indefinite.
   3. The definite article is the, and the indefinite articles are a and an.
   4. The use of articles is very idiomatic.
   5. This is what makes it so hard.
   6. Students whose first language is Spanish, Italian, or French don't have the problems of others.
   7. These languages have more of the same characteristics as the English language.
   8. If a student has problems with articles, listening to the radio will help.
   9. A student should also remember that mastery of a language takes time.
  10. The key to perfection in language learning is practice

Exercise 12:

1. X heroes 2. A situation 3. a hero 4. a lovely 5. the street 6. a two-year 7. an unlocked 8. the toys 9. the backyard 10. a few 11. a small (or the small) 12. the houses 13. the pond 14. the water 15. the water 16. a large 17. The little 18. the house 19. a school 20. X time 21. a break 22. the pond 23. the pond 24. the water 25. the pond 26. the little 27. the water 28. The noise 29. X 30. C.P.R. 31. 911 32. the little 33. A local 34. an article 35. a hero

Exercise 13:

1. a hero 2. the beach 3. a nurse 4. a Chicago 5. a break 6. a beach 7. a hotel 8. the beach 9. the water 10. the beach 11. the emergency 12. a few 13. the sand 14. the water 15. X beach 16. X chairs 17. the blue 18. the beach 19. X protection 20. a hotel 21. the beach 22. the parking 23. a teenage 24. the water 25. the girl 26. the parking 27. the pavement 28. the girl 29. the ground 30. X help 31. a protective 32. the girl 33. a cell 34. X 911 35. the injury 36. the unconscious 37. the paramedics 38. a hero 39. The teenager 40. a huge

Exercise 14: Answers may vary

Exercise 15 A:

1. lands 2. is 3. bloom 4. rent 5. drives 6. gets 7. bump 8. walk 9. brings 10. tell/have 11. laugh 12. are 13. has 14. seems 15. see 16. unpacks 17. go 18. look/begin 19. decide 20. is 21. stand 22. walk 23. spend 24. meets/drives 25. displays 26. fascinate 27. love 28. prefers 29. contains 30. buy 31. decide 32. cover 33. sit 34. recall 35. like 36. stop 37. is 38. represents/need 39. are 40. offers 41. arrive/sit 42. appear 43. head

Exercise 15 B:

1. landed 2. was 3. bloomed 4. rented 5. drove 6. got 7. bumped 8. walked 9. brought 10. told 11. laughed 12. was 13. had 14. seemed 15. saw 16. unpacked 17. went 18. looked/began 19. decided 20. was 21. stood 22. walked 23. spent 24. met/drove 25. displayed 26. fascinated 27. loved 28. preferred 29. contained 30. bought 31 decided 32. covered 33. sat 34. recalled 35. liked 36. stopped 37. was 38. represented/needed 39. were 40. offered 41. arrived/sat 42. appeared 43. headed

Exercise 16:

1. likes 2. work 3. Answers may vary 4. am taking 5. is enjoying, is reading 6. Answers may vary 7. work 8. like 9. meet 10. am serving 11. works

Exercise 17:

1. had 2. was 3. hated 4. wanted 5. were 6. went 7. told 8. seemed 9. visited 10. explained 11. qualifies 12. encouraged 13. offered 14. took 15. discovered

Exercise 18:

1. classes was 2. Rafael was 3. He began 4. he chose 5. He signed 6. These were 7. he enjoyed 8. Rafael noticed 9. he thought 10. He introduced 11. Two were 12. one was 13. quickly became 14. and studied 15. Friends decided 16. They met 17. they had 18. they asked 19. carefully explained 20. They repeated 21. they were 22. them received 23. together gave 24. also made

Exercise 19: Answers may vary

Exercise 20: Answers may vary

Exercise 21 A:

1. built 2. thought/was 3. suggested/should build 4. had retired 5. was 6. was 7. had remarried 8. agreed 9. encouraged 10. began 11. continued 12. built 13. loved 14. watched 15. asked 16. were 17. continued/visited 18. answered 19. was 20. moved/enjoyed

Exercise 21 B: Answers may vary

Exercise 22 A:

Building <u>requires</u>, builder <u>must draw</u>, They <u>have</u>, measurements <u>must be</u>, buyer <u>may ask</u>, builder <u>must make</u>, Builders <u>want</u>, plans <u>are finished</u>/builder <u>applies</u>, permits <u>establish</u>/builder <u>must follow</u>, crew <u>prepares</u>, crew <u>lays</u>, builder <u>must make</u>/workers <u>do</u>, house <u>must pass</u>, amount <u>must be ordered</u>, materials <u>arrive</u>/they <u>must be inspected</u>, Overseeing <u>can be</u>

Bruce <u>enjoys</u>, lumber <u>arrives</u>/he <u>guides</u>, walls <u>are</u>/Bruce <u>can see</u>/house <u>will look</u>, he <u>is</u>, house <u>begins</u>/roof <u>goes</u>, drywall <u>defines</u>, structure <u>begins</u>, homeowners <u>select</u>, They <u>get</u>, This <u>makes</u>/Bruce <u>feel</u>, house <u>is finished</u>, artist <u>plants</u>, it <u>is</u>/family <u>move</u>, it <u>is</u>/crews <u>are working</u>, Building <u>keeps</u>, He <u>will retire</u>, life <u>is</u>/he <u>keeps</u>

Exercise 22 B:

required, had to draw, had, had to be, may have asked, had to make, wanted, were finished, applied, established, had to follow, prepared, laid, had to make, did, had to pass, had to be, arrived, had to be inspected, could be, enjoyed, arrives, guided, were, could see, would look, was, began, went, defined, began, selected, got, made/fill, was finished, planted, was/move, was/were working, kept, would never retire, was, kept

Exercise 22 C:

will require, will draw, will have to be, will ask, will have to make, want (no change), are (no change), will apply, will establish, will have to follow, will prepare, will lay, will be ordered, arrive (no change), will have to be carefully inspected, will be, will enjoy, arrives (no change), is going to guide, will not be complete, will be able to see, will be, will begin, goes on (no change), will define, is really going to begin, will select, will be fixed, will plant, will be, move (no change), will be, are working on (no change), will keep, will never retire, will be exciting, keeps (no change)

Exercise 23:

1. is 2. is 3. are 4. are 5. am/be 6. is 7. is 8. was 9. was 10. were 11. were 12. was 13. was 14. been 15. was 16. is 17. are

Exercise 24: Answers may vary

Exercise 25: Answers may vary

Exercise 26:

1. G <u>spending</u> 2. G <u>Working</u> 3. P <u>looking</u> 4. P <u>hoping</u> 5. G <u>Talking</u> 6. P <u>helping</u> 7. P <u>reaching</u> 8. P <u>running</u> 9. G <u>Grabbing</u> 10. P <u>doing</u> 11. P <u>looking</u> 12. G <u>Looking</u> 13. P <u>getting</u> 14. P <u>acting</u> 15. P <u>going</u> 16. P <u>going</u> 17. P <u>looking</u> 18. P <u>going</u> 19. G <u>selling</u> 20. G <u>Smiling</u> 21. G <u>selling</u> 22. P <u>going</u> 23. G <u>Smiling</u> 24. G <u>Working</u> 25. P <u>taking</u> 26. P <u>shining</u> 27. P <u>beginning</u> 28. G <u>Shop</u>-ping 29. P <u>placing</u> 30. G <u>Turning</u> 31. G <u>understanding</u> 32. P <u>handing</u> 33. G <u>Spending</u> 34. P <u>look</u>-ing 35. P <u>going</u>

Exercise 27:

G	P	P	G	G	G	G	G	P	P	P

<u>Studying</u>, <u>spending</u>, <u>going</u>, <u>Participating</u>, <u>answering</u>, <u>carrying</u>, <u>keeping</u>, <u>happening</u>/<u>finding</u>, <u>trying</u>, <u>going</u>

Exercise 28 A:

P	P	P	G	G	G	P	P	G

<u>finding</u>, <u>sitting</u>, <u>taking</u>, <u>Memorizing</u>/<u>getting</u>, <u>Writing</u>, <u>going</u>, <u>making</u>, <u>getting</u>

Exercise 28 B:

<u>are</u> finding, <u>were</u> sitting, <u>is</u> taking, <u>are</u> not going to require, <u>is</u> taking, <u>is</u> making

Exercise 28 C: Answers may vary

Exercise 29:
1. pleasing 2. filling/enhancing 3. comforting/bracing 4. never-ending 5. invigorating/mouth-watering/ continuing

Exercise 30 A & B:
2. stopping traffic M or C 3. driving fast M 4. honking/screaming D 5. waving a gun M 6. correct 7. carefully approaching M 8. reaching a dangerous M 9. wearing handcuffs M 10. rerouting/ soothing M

Exercise 31:
Answers may vary, but here is a suggestion:
The man wearing a hat, high-heeled shoes, and a dark suit is dancing with a woman wearing a slit skirt and dark, net stockings. The dancing is close and romantic, and the man steps between the feet of the woman curving her leg around his. People watch the dancing couple whirling, dipping, twirling, turning right and turning left. The couple is dancing to sad, crying-like music that comes from an instrument like an accordion called a bandoneon. The dance that is going on now has been going on in Buenos Aires, Argentina, for over a hundred years, and this popular dance is known as the Tango.

Exercise 32:
2. to study correctly/to go 3. to clear/to get/to study 4. To clear/to be looked at 5. to gather/to study 6. to follow 7. to read/to check 8. To read 9. to include 10. to reward 11. to learn 12. to be 13. to follow

Exercise 33:
1. to learn 2. learn 3. to speak 4. to appreciate 5. to live in 6. to visit 7. to enjoy 8. to relax 9. to worry 10. to understand 11. to order 12. to shop 13. need 14. to do 15. to see 16. teach 17. to rely 18. find 19. facing 20. to turn 21. to use 22. to make 23. treat 24. to try 25 to rely 26. Travel (or) Traveling 27. to learn

Exercise 34: Answers may vary

Exercise 35 A:
1. a few 2. a few 3. a little 4. any 5. a few 6. a few 7. a few 8. any 9. A few 10. any 11. a few 12. A few 13. a little 14. a few/a little 15. any 16. a little

Exercise 35 B: Answers may vary, and some cannot be changed smoothly, for example 4, 10, 13.

Exercise 36 A:
1. a little better 2. a few more 3. a few hot 4. a few vegetables 5. a few choices 6. any meat 7. any meat 8. a few 9. a few 10. a little 11. A few

Exercise 36 B:
Answers may vary, but the answers given are those most natural to a native speaker 1. much better 2. many more 3. many/some 4. some 5. many 6. much 7. ANY 8. some/many 9. Some 10. some 11. Some

Exercise 37 A:
1. any 2. some 3. some 4. any 5. some 6. Some 7. any 8. any 9. any 10. Some

Exercise 37 B:
Answers may vary, but the answers given are those most natural to a native speaker 2. Is eating a favorite activity of any students? 3. Do any students enjoy dinner in the college cafeteria? 4. Will they eat any food on their plates? 5. Isn't food the most important thing to some students? 6. Do any students go to the cafeteria to meet other students? 7. Do they enjoy any discussion . . . 8. Do these students talk about any topic except food? 9. Do they sometimes have any new ideas? 10. Do they continue to discuss any of the same old topics?

Exercise 38 A:
1. Any day 2. some new 3. Some workers 4. any workers 5. some other 6. Some of 7. any of 8. some 9. any

Exercise 38 B:
2. They are not adding any new rooms . . . 5. They probably don't work on any other project at that time. 8. They must not have any rules to follow.

Exercise 39 A:
1. This 2. this 3. These 4. These 5. these 6. This 7. this 8. This

Exercise 39 B:
1. These nature programs 2. these programs are showing 6. Those types of activities 7. these facts

Exercise 40:
1. this same 2. these animals 3. this activity 4. these lions 5. these lions 6. this, too 7. these same 8. these interesting

Exercise 41 A:
1. That 2. those 3. Those 4. That 5. those 6. those 7. that 8. those

Exercise 41 B: Answers may vary

Exercise 42:
1. other 2. other 3. another 4. other 5. other 6. Another 7. others 8. Another 9. others 10. other 11. other

Exercise 43:
1. long (cruise) 2. modern (port) 3. large white (ship) 4. interesting (coastline) 5. Green rice (paddies) 6. continuously (worked) 7. happily (waved) 8. slowly (sailed) 9. many unusual (things) 10. Small fishing (boats) 11. Wooden (houseboats) 12. small (space) 13. boat (people) 14. old, large (ships) 15. smaller (boats) 16. quickly (moved)

Exercises 43 B & C: Answers may vary

Exercise 44 A:
talks excitedly, positive attitude, too young, enthusiastically shows/some wartime sites, wonderful Ho Chi Minh City, many shops, delicious fruit/straw hats/colorful clothing, excitedly buy, tall, new buildings, clearly show, fascinating contrasts, happily live

Exercise 44 B: Answers may vary

Exercise 45 A:
large cruise ship/other areas, gentle body, calm river/lovely sights, exotic residence, high walls/necessary protection, totally destroyed, carefully rebuilt, short distance, lovely tombs/small palaces, important cultural center, Vietnamese foreign tourists

Exercise 45 B: Answers may vary

Exercise 46:
1. Finally the 2. probably go 3. beautiful scenery 4. many opportunities 5. easy way 6. clear day 7. ski beautifully 8. easily pass 9. Clearly they 10. more times 11. final analysis

Exercise 47:
1. more interesting than 2. more beautiful paintings 3. the best collection 4. a better tour 5. many details 6. more slowly than 7. much information 8. better than the 9. the most beautiful 10. the funniest I

Exercise 48A:
Answers may vary. Here are suggested answers.
1. important 2. good 3. strong 4. always 5. stressful 6. many 7. frequently 8. sometimes 9. clearly 10. easier

Exercise 48B: Answers may vary

Exercise 49: Answers may vary

Exercise 50 A:
1. He 2. he 3. They 4. She/she 5. She 6. they 7. He 8. He 9. She 10. they 11. He 12. he 13. He/he 14. She 15. she 16. She 17. They

Exercise 50 B:
1. Andre 2. Andre in #1 3. people in #2 4. Aisha 5. Aisha in #4 6. twins 7. Andre 8. Andre 9. Aisha 10. twins in #6 11. Andre 12. Andre in #11 13. Andre in #11 14. Aisha 15. Aisha in #14 16. Aisha in #14 17. children.

Exercise 51:
1. We enjoyed 2. They said 3. He laughed 4. He came 5. He shook 6. he saw 7. he liked 8. He said 9. he jumped 10. They flew 11. they always

Exercise 52 A:
1. They are 2. He lifts 3. She puts 4. She slowly 5. she is 6. he lifts 7. she can 8. She puts 9. They remain 10. He never 11. They both 12. she reaches 13. He swings 14. he gently 15. she removes 16. they leave 17. they bow

Exercise 52 B:
1. They = father and daughter 2. He = father 3. She = daughter 4. She = daughter 5. she = daughter 6. he = father 7. she = daughter 8. She = daughter 9. They = bowls 10. He = father 11. They = father and daughter 12. she = daughter 13. He = father 14. he = father 15. she = daughter 16. they = father and daughter 17. they = father and daughter

Exercise 53 A & B:
1. He—my father 2. He—my father 3. She—Mom 4. She—Mom 5. she—my mother 6. They—the students 7. They—the students 8. He—Dad 9. He—Dad 10. he—Dad 11. he—Dad 12. It—job 13. He—Dad 14. They—Mom and Dad

Exercise 54:
1. they traveled 2. They traveled 3. They learned 4. she discovered 5. They smiled 6. he could 7. they both 8. They had

Exercise 55 A:
1. its 2. them 3. their 4. their 5. his 6. Their 7. them 8. them/their 9. their 10. his 11. his 12. His 13. him 14. his 15. his 16. his 17. us 18. him 19. his/her 20. us

Exercise 55 B:
1. P 2. O 3. P 4. P 5. P 6. P 7. O 8. O/P 9. P 10. P 11. P 12. P 13. O 14. P 15. P 16. P 17. O 18. O 19. P/P 20. O

Exercise 55 C: Answers may vary

Exercise 56 A:
1. It's 2. its 3. It's 4. its 5. It's 6. its 7. its 8. its 9. it's 10. it's

Exercise 56 B: Answers may vary

Exercise 57 A & B:
1. My family-P 2. My father-P 3. His idea-P 4. with him-O 5. to me-O 6. remember them-O 7. My brothers 8. our friends-P 9. My oldest-P 10. at me-O 11. with you-O 12. taught me-O 13. let me 14. to you-O 15. at me-O 16. My ability-P 17. My uncle-P 18. his high-P 19. about him-O 20. His mother-P 21. put them-O 22. of him-O 23. their skills-P 24. use them-O 25. his ability-P 26. His teammates-P 27. her strong-P 28. their goals-P 29. My uncle-P 30. for them-O 31. for him-O

Exercise 58:
1. their 2. her 3. his 4. his 5. her 6. her 7. him 8. his 9. her 10. Her 11. her 12. her 13. him 14. you 15. her 16. them 17. it 18. them

Exercise 59:
1. bore them 2. their minds 3. My partner 4. around us 5. for us 6. our college 7. my friend's 8. his crew 9. his crew 10. His workers 11. called them 12. Their supplier 13. tell me 14. deliver it 15. to us 16. call me 17. their conversation 18. his worker 19. his mind

Exercise 60:
1. our male 2. their girlfriends 3. their boyfriends 4. his girlfriend 5. their conversation 6. telling him 7. at her 8. his eyes 9. to me 10. to me 11. told you 12. to you 13. His eye 14. their behavior 15. bored them 16. Her boyfriend 17. solve it 18. her English 19. about it 20. his comment

Exercise 61:
1. my 2. My 3. My 4. their 5. Their 6. My 7. him 8. He 9. my 10. He 11. I 12. He 13. their 14. my 15. its (or her) 16. your 17. she 18. her 19. It 20. he

Exercise 62:
1. my parents 2. It was 3. It was 4. it was 5. My parents 6. they could 7. They loved 8. his free 9. his garden 10. his garden

Exercise 63:
1. make it 2. its citizens 3. their homes 4. they need 5. they usually 6. their customers 7. their needs 8. makes it 9. they don't

Exercise 64:
1. themselves 2. himself 3. himself 4. herself 5. himself 6. himself 7. himself 8. yourself 9. herself 10. themselves 11. himself 12. himself 13. yourself 14. themselves 15. himself 16. himself 17. himself

Exercise 65:
1. get themselves 2. by herself 3. by herself 4. by herself 5. keep themselves 6. got herself 7. dress herself 8. over herself 9. to herself 10. by yourself 11. by herself

Exercise 66:
1. of themselves 2. by himself 3. by himself 4. by themselves 5. drove herself 6. drove herself 7. by himself 8. by yourself

Exercise 67:

1. himself-I 2. himself-C 3. himself-I 4. himself-E 5. himself-C 6. herself-E 7. themselves-C 8. themselves-E 9. himself-I 10. yourself-I 11. myself-I 12. ourselves-E 13. themselves-C 14. himself-C 15. himself-I 16. themselves-C

Exercise 68:

1. by himself 2. for himself 3. hides himself 4. among themselves 5. know yourselves 6. to himself 7. get myself 8. to ourselves 9. by himself

Exercise 69 A & B:

1. they should-S 2. they have-S 3. their arrival-P 4. by themselves-R 5. join them-O 6. They want-S 7. of himself-R 8. of myself-R

Exercise 70:

1. They-Mary and Paul 2. It-Maui 3. She-Mary 4. he-Paul 5. him-Paul 6. he-Paul 7. their-Paul and Mary 8. They-Paul and Mary, 9. they-Paul and Mary 10. themselves-Paul and Mary

Exercise 71:

1. who 2. that 3. who, 4. that 5. that 6. that, 7. who, 8. which, 9. who, 10. whom

Exercise 72 A:

1. that serve 2. that set 3. which is 4. Wish the 5. that is 6. who never 7. that the 9. that burned 10. that comes

Exercise 72 B:

2. He likes tacos with chilis. The chilis set his mouth on fire. 3. Indian curry is hot and spicy. Indian curry makes him smile. 4. If John gets pizza, he adds red pepper. The waiter brings the red pepper to the table. 5. He must have a stomach. The stomach is strong. 6. John is a person. A person never gets sick from food. 7. He can eat everything. The waiter brings everything. 8. X, 9. He brought some peppers. The peppers burned our tongues. 10. We love the smell. The smell comes out of the microwave into the hall.

Exercise 73:

1. The food called Tex-Mex, which I like, is spicy. 2. Students who need money for tuition can apply for work-study scholarships. 3. She asked to see the dress that was in the store's window. 4. Thomas Jefferson who was an American statesman had many other interests. 5. She is the friend who always gets me into trouble. 6. I shared my idea, which was simple. 7. The Civil War was an unpopular war that was really motivated by greed. 8. The movie which is well known all over the world is *Star Wars*. 9. The basket was full of newspapers that were old. 10. They are the people whom (that) I told you about.

Exercise 74:

1. in 1995-in 2. by the public school-by 3. in the evening-in 4. of the students-of 5. in my class-in 6. from other countries-from 7. to class-to 8. with my husband-with 9. for his co-workers-for 10. at his office-at

Exercise 75:

1. At 2. in 3. In 4. in 5. in 6. in 7. at 8. on 9. in 10. in 11. at 12. in 13. on 14. in 15. in 16. in 17. in 18. at 19. on 20. in

Exercise 76 B: Answers may vary

Exercise 77:

Answers may vary. Here are suggested answers.

1. Did John have a business trip? 2. Did he travel on Tuesday? 3. Was the weather bad that day? 4. Was John's flight delayed one hour? 5. Could the plane fly in the storm? 6. Did John spend time reading a comic book? 7. Did he fall asleep while he was reading? 8. Did John hear the announcement to board his flight? 9. Did John's flight leave without him? 10. Did John have to go to the ticket counter to ask for a new ticket?

Exercise 78:

Answers may vary. Here are suggested answers.

1. Who had a business trip? 2. When did he travel? 3. What was the weather like that day? 4. Whose flight was delayed one hour? 5. Why couldn't the plane fly? 6. How did John spend time? 7. When did John fall asleep? 8. What didn't John hear? 9. Whose flight left without him? 10. Where did John have to go to ask for a new ticket?

Exercise 79: Answers may vary

Exercise 80:

1. Jung didn't believe 2. He didn't describe 3. He didn't look 4. Some people aren't 5. They don't talk and move 6. They don't get 7. They don't ask 8. Extroverted students don't jump 9. Other people aren't 10. They don't talk less and aren't less 11. They don't get 12. They aren't excellent 13. Introverts don't like to 14. Introverts don't avoid 15. Introverts and extroverts aren't quite

Exercise 81 A:

(contractions are provided, but the complete word is acceptable, for example, do not, does not) ~~is~~ isn't, ~~have~~ don't have (**or** haven't), ~~pay~~ don't pay; ~~can~~ can't, ~~prefer~~ don't prefer, ~~need~~ don't need, ~~want~~ don't want, ~~is~~ isn't, ~~may have~~ may not have, ~~are~~ aren't, ~~find~~ don't find; ~~can~~ can't, ~~come~~ don't come, ~~like~~ don't like, ~~comes~~ doesn't come, ~~show~~ don't show, ~~are~~ aren't, ~~can cause~~ can't cause, ~~need~~ don't need

Exercise 81 B: Answers may vary

Exercise 82 A:

1. comes from 2. rely on 3. deal with 4. look at 5. fall in 6. relies on 7. side of 8. go to 9. end of 10. are in 11. come from 12. everything to 13. happening in 14. looking at 15. life with 16. isn't in 17. Students in 18. wasn't on 19. perception of 20. involved in 21. anything on 22. watches on 23. time in 24. come to 25. say to 26. come to

Exercise 82 B: Answers may vary

Exercise 83 A & B:

1. (D) <u>is not</u>-main verb 2. (I) X 3. (M) didn't (helping) know (main) 4. (I) X 5. (D) don't (helping) have (main) 6. (D) have (helping) NEVER (adverb) voted (main) 7. (I) X 8. (I) X 9 (E) can't (helping) believe (main) 10. (D) don't (helping) believe (main) 11. (I) Don't (helping) have to (main) 12. (I) 13. (I) 14. (D) have not (helping) been (main)

Exercise 83 C:

Answers may vary, but here are samples: 1. A presidential race in the United States is not always a pretty sight, and . . . 2. Although we have other political parties, these minor parties usually don't have much effect on . . . 3. I have never voted for any party other than Republican or Democrat because I rarely know the other candidates.

Exercise 83 D: Answers may vary

Glossary

adjective Any of a group of words that limits, qualifies, or modifies nouns. Adjectives in English generally come before the nouns they modify. *For example, "She was a good cat."* (The word "good" modifies cat.)

adverb Any of a group of words that modifies verbs, adjectives, or other adverbs, by expressing time, place, manner, degree, cause, and so on. *For example, "Grandfather walked slowly around the block."* (The word "slowly" is an adverb telling how he walked.)

affirmative The opposite of negative, an affirmative statement is positive; it means yes instead of no. *For example, "I will complete my degree by May of next year."* (Instead of meaning that the degree will not be finished, the speaker affirms that the outcome will be positive. If questioned, he or she would say, "yes.")

antecedent The word, phrase, or clause to which a pronoun refers in a sentence or clause. *For example, "I helped my mother wash her hair when she was sick."* (The words "her" and "she" both refer to the noun, "mother.") Another word for antecedent is **referent.**

antonyms Words with opposite meanings. *For example, hot/cold, here/there, yes/no, accept/reject.*

article A word placed before a noun to show whether the noun is used in a particular or general way. Articles are the words "a," "an," and "the." "A" is called **the indefinite article** because it is used in a general way. It becomes "an" before a vowel or silent "h"; "the" is the **definite article** because it is used to indicate a particular noun rather than a general one. *For example, "I bought the can of beans that was on sale."* (This is a particular brand of beans.) *I bought a can of beans.* (This is any can of beans.)

auxiliary verbs Or helping verbs, these words are joined to a principal verb to express action or state as to manner or time, to indicate the mood or tense in which it is used. *For example, "My uncle **is** running for mayor, and I **am** betting that he **will** win."* (The words in bold are helping verbs.)

clause A group of words containing a subject and verb that may or may not be a complete sentence. A clause may be "independent," which makes it a sentence, or it may be "dependent," which makes it a subordinate clause. *For example, "They wrote it down."* (Sentence) *"Although I put on my turn signal . . ."* (Dependent clause).

colon Punctuation (:) used to indicate a list following an independent clause. It also joins two independent clauses in order to show a very close cause/effect relationship.

comma Punctuation (,), frequently called "half stop," used in various sentence constructions in English.

complex sentence A sentence composed of one independent clause and a dependent clause. *For example, "If garbage day falls on a holiday, they will collect it the next day."* The first word group written before the comma is the dependent clause, and the word group after the comma is the independent clause. It may also be written: *"They will collect the garbage the next day if garbage day falls on a holiday."* (Notice the difference in the use of the comma.)

compound sentence A sentence composed of two independent clauses connected by a conjunction. *For example, "She really wanted to meet us in the park, but her brother needed the car."*

count nouns Substantives that can be used in either a singular or a plural form when broken down into their integral parts. *For example, "The man bought three **suits**."* (For the opposite of count nouns, refer to noncount nouns.)

dangling modifier A modifying phrase that fails to make a clear connection with a noun or other word it seeks to modify. *For example, "Walking across the creek, the shoe fell in the water.* (The person who was wearing the shoe was "walking across the creek," but that connection isn't clear because the word "person" is not in the sentence.)

declarative One of the four types of sentence structures, this in the form of a statement, not a command, an exclamation, or a question, and punctuated at the end with a period. *For example, "My wife's job is mentally challenging."*

demonstrative A type of modifier that points out its noun. *For example, "These people have dinner reservations for eight o'clock."* (The demonstratives in English are "this," "that," "these," "those." The first two are for singular nouns, and the last two are for use with plural nouns.)

exclamatory One of the four types of sentence structures, this is the form of an emotional utterance, end-punctuated by the exclamation mark(!). *For example, "How wonderful your party was!"*

fanboys A device used in this workbook to help us recall the coordinating conjunctions. The fanboys are *for, and, nor, but, or, yet, so.*

gerund A verb ending in -ing that has all the characteristics of a noun, but may retain some of its verbal functions as well, such as the ability to take an object or an adverbial modifier. *For example, "**Doing** a job well is laudable."* ("Doing" is normally thought of as a verb, such as, "I am doing the best I can!" although here, it is in the subject position and is a noun.)

helping verbs See **auxiliary verbs.**

homonyms Words that are pronounced the same but spelled differently and that have different meanings. *For example, too/to/two, there/their/they're, here/hear.*

idiomatic verbs/expressions Stemming from the word "idiom," which means the distinctive language or dialect of a people or region, idiomatic verbs and expressions often represent a major change in the meaning perceived from the verb itself. Idiomatic expressions must be understood from their connotations rather than from their strict denotations. *For example, the idiomatic verb phrase, "I give up," means to surrender.* (The verb, "give," while it has many meanings, hardly provides us with a clue as to its significance in this phrase.)

imperative One of the four types of sentence structures in which a command or strong request is given in a supplicating or demanding manner, very often with the subject omitted as it is "understood" to be "you." *For example, "Get out of here." "Please help me."*

interjection A word or words used to signify emotion. Various parts of speech are used as interjections. *For example, "Great!"*

interrogative One of the four types of sentence structures in which a question is asked. The interrogative may be a simple question, one that can be answered by a simple yes or no: *Example, "Is the train on time?"* Or the interrogative may be a wh-question whose answer is not a simple yes or no *Example: "What time will the train arrive?" "Who knows the answer?" "Whose car is parked in front of the house?" "Where did you buy those earrings?"*

irregular verbs Verbs whose endings and/or roots change in the three tense forms, as opposed to those that are regular. (See **regular verbs.**) *For example, the present tense of break is* **break,** *the past tense is* **broke,** *and the participle form is* **broken.**

limiting words In the context of this workbook, limiting words are those words that will indicate whether to use plural or singular. *For example, "I asked for a lot of potatoes with my lunch."* (**A lot of** tells the reader/writer that the noun following will be plural unless it is a noncount noun.)

misplaced modifier A word, phrase, or clause that follows a word in a sentence that is not the word the modifier means to change or augment. *For example, "He drank the water out of the old bucket that was purified with chlorine."* (The bucket is not purified, but the water is. The modifier "that was purified with chlorine" is too far away from the word "water" for it to have the modifying meaning it strives for.)

modal A class of auxiliary or helping verbs that are used to change subtly the meaning of the verb: may, can, could, might, would, and others.

modifier A word, phrase, or clause that changes or augments the meaning of another word or phrase, an adjective, or adverb. *For example, "The* **big, angry** *dog ran* **quickly** *toward me."* (The first two bold words are modifiers called adjectives and the third is an adverb. Adjectives and adverbs are modifiers.)

negative The opposite of positive, as in denial or saying no. In grammar, we use negative to mean a word or sentence that expresses refusal, denial, or negation. *For example, "The river did* **not** *overflow its banks in spite of the flood."* (The word **not** changes the verb as well as the sentence's meaning to negative.)

noncount nouns Names of people, places, and/or things that remain the same in their singular and plural forms since they cannot be separated out or divided. *For example, "I put some* **gasoline** *in my car today."* (Although we could count gallons of gasoline, we cannot separate out and count "gasoline," so it, along with most liquids, is a noncount noun.)

noun One of the parts of speech in English, it is the name of any person, place, or thing, of anything we can see, hear, feel, or touch, or anything of which we can have any idea or notion. It is often called "substantive." Here are two classes of nouns—**proper noun** and **common noun.** A proper noun is the name of a particular person, place, thing, or group of persons, places, or things. *For example, "***George Washington** *is known as the father of our country,* **the United States.***"* (The words in bold are proper nouns.) A common noun is the name of any one of a class or group. *For example, "***Teachers** *are the most underpaid* **group** *of public* **servants.***"* (The words in bold are common nouns.) Nouns are distinguished by having four properties: gender, person, number, and case.

object A word or words used in the object position in a sentence, that is, as direct object after a verb, as indirect object, as object of a preposition, a word in the objective case. *For example, "The woman in the department store gave* **me a sample** *to try."* (The word "me" in this sentence is the indirect object and the word "sample" is the direct object.)

participial A word or phrase derived from a verb and used as a noun or adjective. *"For example, "He opened his speech, calling for more support from his home state."* (The phrase, beginning with "calling . . ." is a participial phrase.)

participle A word that is made from a verb, participates in the properties of a verb and of an adjective or noun. Two participles are formed directly from the stem of a verb, the present and the past participle: *loving and loved.* The present participle always ends in -*ing* and implies a continuation of an action. The past or perfect participle implies a completion of action, state, or being.

phrasal verbs See **idiomatic verbs/expressions.**

phrase A group of two or more words conveying a single thought or forming a separate part of a sentence but not containing a subject and predicate. *For example, "to the lighthouse. . . ."*

plural Refers to more than one of something. *For example, "***Dogs*** are man's best* ***friends,*** *and sometimes they are the best* ***friends*** *to* ***women,*** *too."* (The bold words are plural, meaning more than one.)

possessive Indicates possession or ownership. *For example, "This is* ***his*** *book. That other one is* ***Robert's*** *book. I have* ***mine*** *here, and* ***yours*** *is on the table."*

predicate The word or words that make a statement about the subject in a clause or sentence. *For example, "The babysitter took the children to the park and later to McDonald's for a snack before nap time."* (All the words following "The babysitter" comprise the predicate of the sentence.)

preposition A part of speech that serves to connect words and show the relationships between objects which the words express. Three classes of prepositions are simple, compound, complex.

referent See **antecedent.**

reflexive A form of a pronoun that refers to the antecedent, a pronoun used as the direct object of a verb. *For example, "I wash* ***myself*** *daily."*

regular verbs Verb whose forms follow a consistent pattern of change for each of the three tenses. Tenses in English are generally regular. *For example, "The verb* ***wrap*** *changes its form in this manner: present tense-***wrap***; past tense adds "ed"-***wrapped***, participle form also adds "ed"-have* ***wrapped.***

relative pronoun A form of a pronoun that relates to an antecedent, that is, a preceding noun or phrase, and introduces a dependent clause qualifying or limiting the antecedent. Relative pronouns are *who, which, that, what. For example, "He is the teacher that you met last week."*

simple sentence A sentence containing one independent clause. *For example, "The twenty-first century is upon us."*

singular Refers to only one. *For example, "A* ***poet*** *once said that a* ***baby*** *is God's* ***opinion*** *that the* ***world*** *should go on."* (All the words in bold are singular because they indicate only one of something.)

semicolon A common punctuation mark (;), used to join two independent clauses or to separate items in a list when a comma is already being used within the items, or used in front of correlative conjunctions to compound sentences.

subject A sentence's or clause's subject is a word or group of words about which something is said, or what the sentence is about. A subject is always a noun or pronoun. *For example, "Children are naturally energetic."* (The noun, children, is the subject of the sentence, the subject of the verb energetic.)

subordinate conjunction A word which, it not attached to an independent clause, cuases a clause to be dependent and consequently an incomplete sentence. For example, "Because it snowed last night..." The word because is a subordinate conjunction because it makes this clause dependent, a fragment.

synonyms Words whose meanings are the same or nearly the same. *For example, "scream/yell, say/tell, car/automobile."*

tense The property of a verb that expresses action, being, or state concerning time. In English, three great divisions of time are past, present, and future. The **present tense** denotes the moment that is now. *For example, "The dog barks."* The **past tense** denotes time in the past; it is also called the "preterit" or "imperfect." *For example, "Yesterday, the dog barked."* The **future tense** refers to time after the present, in the future. *For example, "The dog will bark tomorrow."* (These are called the **simple tenses**.) To these simple tenses, we add the *-ing* participle form of the main verb and a **helping verb** (is/are/was/were) to make the continuous or progressive tenses. *For example, "They are running away from home."* English speakers also use the **perfect tenses** quite a lot. They are as follows: present perfect (has or have + past participle), past perfect (had + past participle), future perfect (will + have + past participle) along with their corresponding **continuous** or **progressive** tenses (has/have/had/will have + been + participle + ing). *For example, "She has been having a great deal of trouble with her algebra class lately."*

Write your own new VOCABULARY WORDS here.